designing with light
hotels

RotoVision

design wi

designed by keith lovegrove

hotels

ing

th light

jill entwistle

A RotoVision Book

Published and distributed by RotoVision SA

Rue du Bugnon 7

CH-1299 Crans-Près-Céligny

Switzerland

RotoVision SA, Sales & Production Office

Sheridan House, 112/116A Western Road

Hove, East Sussex BN3 1DD, UK

Tel: +44 (0) 1273 72 72 68

Fax: +44 (0) 1273 72 72 69

E-mail: sales@rotovision.com

Website: www.rotovision.com

Distributed to the trade in the United States by:

Watson-Guptill Publications

1515 Broadway

New York, NY 10036

10 9 8 7 6 5 4 3 2 1

ISBN 2-88046-447-1

Book design by Lovegrove Associates

Production and separations in Singapore by ProVision Pte. Ltd.

Tel: +65 334 7720

Fax: +65 334 7721

acknowledgements

The author, editor and publisher would like to thank the following companies for their contributions to this book: Jonathan Speirs and Associates, Kai Piippo, Maurice Brill Lighting Design, Licht Kunst Licht, The Flaming Beacon, Francis Krahe and Associates, Dirk Obliers Design, United Designers, Concord Lighting, Olga Polizzi, Lighting Design International, Lighting Planners Associates, Ross De Alessi Lighting Design, Isometrix, and Lockington.

Special thanks go to Sally Storey of Lighting Design International, Maurice Brill of Maurice Brill Lighting Design, Jonathan Speirs of Jonathan Speirs and Associates, and David Kerr of Dynalite.

A big thanks also to Nick Hoggett of DPA Lighting Consultants.

My appreciation to designer Keith Lovegrove for bringing out the best of both words and pictures, and particular thanks to editor Natalia Price-Cabrera for her exceptional patience.

Jill Entwistle
London, 2000

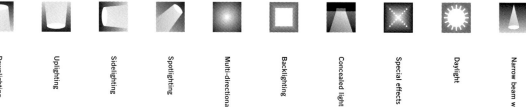

Downlighting

Uplighting

Sidelighting

Spotlighting

Multi-directional lighting

Backlighting

Concealed lighting

Special effects

Daylight

Narrow beam width

Medium beam width

Broad beam width

Alongside the images featured in this book, the symbols above describe the type of directional lighting used, with the beam widths as appropriate.
These symbols relate to the main lighting system in the relevant illustration.

contents

intro

section one

'A hotel is a 24-hour economy in which each guest determines his own pace. While one guest sleeps, another eats, a third works, a fourth arrives and a fifth checks out,' Ron Kaal wrote in an article for *Frame* magazine.

The hotel has often been perceived as a universe in microcosm, a city within a city. Guests work, eat and sleep there, they hold meetings, they do deals, they socialise, they take a sauna, they spend their honeymoon, they commit adultery. Some people are there because they have to be and some because they have saved a lifetime for it. The hotel may be a substitute home or the ultimate escape from the dreariness of home routine.

Amanusa, Bali. COURTESY OF NATHAN THOMPSON/THE FLAMING BEACON.   Four Seasons, New York, USA. COURTESY OF COLUMBUS COMMUNICATIONS.   Mondrian Hotel, Los Angeles, USA. COURTESY OF PHILIPPE STARCK.

It is nevertheless an unreal world. There is as much an air of artifice about the hotel environment as there is about the names Mr and Mrs Smith in the register. Life does not run smoothly 24 hours a day but in a hotel it must. Whether the establishment is internationally anonymous (check out the book of matches for where you are) or idiosyncratically charming, it is a stage set.

'Hotels, restaurants and bars are the closest thing to theatre in the real world,' says Jonathan Speirs of the Lighting Architects Group (Jonathan Speirs and Associates/Speirs and Major). Like any stage set, the design can be as minimal or as baroque as the brief (or historical reputation) dictates. But whether it twinkles like an old dowager's tiara or glows with minimalist subtlety, it is the lighting which invests the hotel with atmosphere. Like any stage set, the hotel needs illumination to achieve animation. As hotels become bolder and braver in design terms and technology continues to evolve, the opportunities to exploit the possibilities of lighting are more exciting than they have ever been.

When it comes to public arenas, hotels have arguably led the way in good lighting. 'The main hotel groups were aware of lighting earlier than most other people and have been fundamental in the growth of lighting designers,' says Maurice Brill of Maurice Brill Lighting Design.

'The hotelier truly understands the difference between good and bad lighting,' says Jonathan Speirs. 'One general manager said to me years ago, if there's a downlight out it's a reflection on me. I've never heard a shopping centre manager say that.'

The 24-hour usage, the multiplicity of activities (from bathroom to ballroom), the complexity of spaces which may play more than one role – all these factors have massive implications for the lighting. In conjunction with the architecture and interior design, it is called on to fulfil a wide variety of demands: it makes guests feel welcome and comfortable; it signals image and marketing position; it designates and differentiates zones; it helps guests to navigate in an unfamiliar space; it governs their safety. Ultimately, it creates the ambience and sets the tone.

Dan Hotel, Eilat, Israel. COURTESY OF FOCUS LIGHTING. PHOTOGRAPH © RAMI ARNOLD.

Grand Hyatt, Muscat. COURTESY OF HANCOCK COMMUNICATIONS.

Asahi, Tokyo, Japan. COURTESY OF PHILIPPE STARCK.

The lobby: Setting the scene

The lobby is where guests register and where the hotel registers with them. Their initial impression gained from the exterior will be reinforced – or not – when they enter through the revolving door. This impression is important not only in satisfying resident guests but also in attracting potential guests or corporate clients who may be there just for a business meeting or social occasion. 'You need to generate warmth and a sense of excitement,' says Maurice Brill. 'It also wants to be a space that is fairly easy to negotiate without too much need for signage, so that you can find your way to things like the lift lobby, the reception and so on. It's a combination of warmth, comfort, drama, enticement and ease of navigation.'

The atmosphere will also be dependent on the time of day. It must feel equally appropriate for the person checking out for an early morning flight as the guest looking for a post-prandial cognac at midnight. 'You're not changing the interior, but you're changing the mood and that is fundamentally done by the lighting,' says Sally Storey of Lighting Design International. 'In the morning you want things sharper and crisper. In the evening you want to create that unwinding feeling.'

Alternatively, depending on the nature of the hotel, the evening mood might be more upbeat. 'At night a lot of these hotels have major balls or functions and they don't want the lobby too sleepy,' says Nick Hoggett of DPA Lighting Consultants. 'The lighting is an important component in reinforcing grandeur, creating a sense of somewhere special.'

Against the ambient backcloth, focal points will both give the space visual texture and help guests orientate themselves. 'You think of the design in terms of a number of important blocks,' says Jonathan Speirs. 'The first big block is what message are you trying to get across, you should think about prioritising the space. Obviously the reception is kind of important, but there might be a feature that's more important – a major piece of sculpture in the middle of the atrium floor, for instance. This applies to all areas. It's not to do with lighting, it's to do with

vision, what you want the eye drawn to.'

While navigation is primarily a design function, it is one which can be very effectively augmented by lighting. The eye is automatically attracted to areas of higher brightness. 'When you enter a space you want to make a dramatic focus so your eye is immediately drawn to something,' says Sally Storey. 'Light the threshold and then light something beyond the threshold to draw you into the space and welcome you in. Typically you might have flowers by the reception desk and that would be the focus.'

Lobby ceiling with pyramidal skylight at the Fukuoka Hyatt Regency Hotel and Office Building, Fukuoka, Japan (overleaf). COURTESY OF MICHAEL GRAVES & ASSOCIATES, INC. PHOTOGRAPH © YOSHIYA TOYOTA COURTESY OF MAEDA CORPORATION.

Oulton Hall, Leeds, UK. COURTESY OF MAURICE BRILL LIGHTING DESIGN. PHOTOGRAPH BY MALCOLM RUSSELL.

Wasserturm Hotel, Cologne, Germany. PHOTOGRAPH BY DEIDI VON SCHAEWEN.

Tea Lounge at the Hong Kong Park View, Hong Kong. COURTESY OF LIGHT DIRECTIONS LTD.

Oulton Hall, Leeds, UK. COURTESY OF MAURICE BRILL LIGHTING DESIGN. PHOTOGRAPH BY MALCOLM RUSSELL.

Reception

The reception is both a practical and decorative element. On a functional level the lighting has to fulfil a number of criteria. Downlighting positioned over the desktop will ensure that guests can see what they are signing. Similarly some form of illumination must be considered for staff behind the desk to perform their tasks. The use of monitors means that care needs to be taken to avoid glare falling on VDU screens or, for that matter, in the eyes of staff and guests – and that includes reflected glare from shiny materials.

The space must look welcoming – with warm sources, invariably tungsten halogen, and perhaps wallwashing or projection on the wall behind the desk. Staff must be clearly discernible and look attractive. (Some rules, of course, are made to be broken in the more avant-garde environment. At London's desperately stylish Hempel, for example, staff behind the desk are deliberately kept in silhouette). Guests must also appear in a flattering light – some form of illumination at face height (such as table lamps) softens the effect of the downlighting. Neither must be subject to unflattering shadowing by badly positioned downlighting – 'That's a common mistake that gets made,' says Maurice Brill.

Depending on whether or not the reception desk is to be the primary element in the space (and hi-tech developments such as automatic check out will affect that), it can be played up or down. According to the design and the materials used, fibre optic uplighting at the base, or the incorporation of cold cathode, for example, would give decorative emphasis. 'There is a tendency with some groups not to over accentuate the reception – they feel it should be there but not be the principal focus. Others feel differently,' says Brill. 'We would try to generate something that had a quiet sense of drama and accent to it. If we could we'd have an underlit glass counter or some accented flowers or sculpture, or silhouetted panels – things that catch the eye and say look over here.'

Lobby/Lounge bar

In larger hotels the open plan expanse of the lobby is actually a series of spaces – reception, accounts desk (if separate), concierge's desk, route through to the lift lobby, shop, a lounge area, bar and so on. Here lighting is a useful tool in defining boundaries where material walls are absent.

'I think you want to create a clear route that defines the area to the reception desk, and then it's good if you can show other areas either side having different moods,' says Sally Storey. 'You'll sometimes have areas of darkness in between which effectively become your walls and then lit areas beyond which are your "rooms". You create divides so that you feel you are walking into different spaces and they have different draws. You're creating a sense of individuality for spaces.'

The imposing table lamps in lounge areas are becoming less obligatory but are nevertheless a useful device – for introducing a human scale in a soaring space, for providing flattering side-lighting to people's faces and as a cipher of domestic comforts. However, that sense of cosy domesticity – always somewhat contrived – is gradually being supplanted by a more dramatic approach. 'People like Philippe Starck are creating the theatre set and I believe that's the way more and more hotels will go – generating excitement and a space that people will marvel at and talk about,' says Maurice Brill.

Four Seasons, New York, USA. COURTESY OF COLUMBUS COMMUNICATIONS.

Belfry Hotel, Wishaw, UK. COURTESY OF MAURICE BRILL LIGHTING DESIGN. PHOTOGRAPH BY ROBIN HEAD.

Lifts/Lift lobby: light transport

The transition to back of house generally has perhaps been paid less attention than it might – after all, waiting for a lift gives people ample time to assess their surroundings. Ill-considered lighting can alternatively mean a gloomy ride to the room, or one where the downlighting half blinds the occupants as it bounces its way round reflective surfaces designed to counter claustrophobia. (Where the latter is concerned, bright ceilings make the cabin look higher while illuminated wall panels will also increase the sense of space.)

Recent lighting schemes have given the lift lobby more drama with the simple device of buried uplights rather than a reliance on downlights. In the case of London's One Aldwych, that was taken a step further with the use of fibre optics to edge-light the base and top of the glass lift to create a green glow in the morning and a purple tint at night.

'You want the lighting to be directed away from people waiting for the lift rather than have those "beam me up Scottie downlights" directly overhead,' says Sally Storey. 'I would tend to light a sculpture or artwork so that people have got something visually interesting to look at. I would also position fittings at the lift front rather than just generally in the centre.'

Inside the lift the decorative possibilities can range from the more glitzy use of fibre optics in the ceiling to lighting the handrail or even an underlit floor. 'We always regard the lift lobby and lift as spaces to be dealt with rather than an aside to everything else, but quite simply too because it's not an area that people want to spend too much money on,' says Brill.

Light tunnel, Pflaums Posthotel Pegnitz, Germany (left, overleaf). COURTESY OF DICK OBLIERS DESIGN.
Paramount, New York, USA (far right, overleaf). COURTESY OF PHILIPPE STARCK.

Lindrum, Melbourne, Australia. COURTESY OF THE FLAMING BEACON. PHOTOGRAPH © PETER HYATT.

Hotel Square, Paris, France. COURTESY OF COLUMBUS COMMUNICATIONS.

Oulton Hall, Leeds, UK. COURTESY OF MAURICE BRILL LIGHTING DESIGN. PHOTOGRAPH BY MALCOLM RUSSELL.

Corridors: light of passage

The corridor is another of those transitional spaces that has perhaps suffered from a lack of attention, but as The Point in Edinburgh amply demonstrates (see page 36), it has a great deal of potential as a dramatic space. As one lighting designer pointed out, given that the rooms are where hoteliers make their money, the least they could do is make the approach to them more interesting.

For what is apparently a straightforward space, in lighting terms there are a number of factors to consider, not least of which is that there is usually no natural light at all. The corridors must be lit 24 hours a day which has both aesthetic and energy implications. A control system is essential – as it is in just about every area of a hotel – so that appropriate light levels can be created for different stages of the day. Guests are unlikely to appreciate eyeball stabbing brightness at three in the morning or a murky start to the day. Different scene settings will also make it possible to switch between sources. 'In the late evening you might just leave the doors lit,' says Sally Storey, 'so the whole mood at two or three in the morning is rather dramatic.' Other theatrical touches include pinspotting or backlighting room numbers, and using low level uplighting along corridor walls.

Clearly there are safety considerations which mean minimum illumination must be maintained, but dipping down levels will also considerably reduce energy consumption. While for energy saving reasons compact fluorescents have become more acceptable in areas such as corridors, there are still two schools of thought as to its appropriateness in top-end hotels. 'Whether you use compact fluorescents depends on the star rating of the hotel. You might use a compact for general lighting, from a wall light for instance,' says Storey.

'To use a CFL (compact fluorescent lighting) with the much better colour rendering that exists now in places such as corridors isn't a bad thing, especially bearing in mind that they're probably going to be running 24 hours a day,' maintains Jonathan Speirs.

Anonymous corridors are easily invested with a menacing quality. A solution strictly based on downlighting is likely to produce shadowing and increase the difficulty of discerning facial features, not a reassuring scenario. Lighting vertical surfaces will also make the passage appear less claustrophobic and threatening. If the corridor is long, and they invariably are, it is also important to break up that length.

'The worst thing about a corridor is it can look as if it goes on for ever and in a way you want to use the lighting to foreshorten it,' says Storey. 'You may just illuminate the entrances to the rooms – with a wall light or a downlight – and you might combine that with a coffer light or a pendant. Every now and then it helps to provide a visual stop to the lighting by lighting something on the side, such as a piece of artwork or a floral arrangement.'

elix Restaurant, The Peninsula, Hong Kong. COURTESY OF PHILIPPE STARCK.

Fifty Seven Fifty Seven Bar & Restaurant Oculus, Four Seasons Hotel, New York, USA. COURTESY OF COLUMBUS COMMUNICATIONS.

Lindrum, Melbourne, Australia. COURTESY OF THE FLAMING BEACON. PHOTOGRAPH © PETER HYATT.

Restaurants/bars: sources for courses

'If you expect people to use hotel facilities there's no point creating universal blandness and boredom. They have to mimic the high street effect where people feel they have a choice of venues,' says Maurice Brill. 'The reason people feel that is because they're not all designed or lit in the same manner. The hotel should be designed in that way too.'

While maintenance considerations are a key issue in hotel lighting schemes, the dogmatic use of the same fitting requiring the same lamp in a series of venues for convenience and cost reasons can create uniformity and insipidness.

At the other end of the spectrum is the trend to create an individual, independent profile for hotel bars and restaurants, giving them separate entrances and psychologically divorcing them from the hotel environment. In many southeast Asian countries, where fine dining has long been associated with hotels rather than independent restaurants, it is an established tradition to view the restaurant as an entity in its own right rather than just as a hotel facility.

Whatever the nature of the venue, the social element is at the heart of the wining/dining experience. How people are made to look and feel by the lighting is paramount. It should be flattering to faces (warm sources and ideally balanced from above and from the sides to avoid harsh shadows). It should create a conducive atmosphere, for which a control system is vital and nowhere more so than the hotel outlet which is breakfast, lunch and dinner venue.

Lighting must make the space visually stimulating. One of the reasons customers fail to linger in the overbright, uniform lighting of fast food outlets is that visual monotony causes fatigue. With layers of lighting – accenting of artworks or floral arrangements, wallwashing, concealed lighting in coves or behind banquettes, low level uplighting, back- or edge-lighting of glass elements, backlit or cold cathode trimmed bars – rather than an overemphasis on downlighting, the space becomes more sculpted, more interesting, more three-dimensional.

The bar or restaurant is also an opportunity to apply more theatrical techniques such as colour change projectors and gobos. Even in restrained interior schemes, coloured light projections or washes can be a dynamic decorative element, especially effective in countering the coldness of a large space.

Sea Bar, St Martins Lane, London, UK (overleaf). COURTESY OF ISOMETRIX. PHOTOGRAPH © TODD EBERLE.

Amandari, Bali. COURTESY OF NATHAN THOMPSON/THE FLAMING BEACON.

Hotel Atelier Sul Mare, Italy. COURTESY OF ANTONIO PRESTI.

Metropolitan Hotel, London, UK. COURTESY OF UNITED DESIGNERS.

Rooms: for improvement

While the formulaic approach to international hotels is being challenged, the one area which has been slowest to change is the room itself. One reason is the forces of conservatism. Hoteliers unnerved by the idea of upsetting their clientele with anything too *outré* are doubly concerned about the room which is the nub of the hotel experience. The inoffensive colour schemes and attempt to recall domesticity in the shape of traditional table and standard lamps have therefore persisted in many establishments.

Budget is the other constraint. Where an extravagance might be permissible in public areas, the addition of, say, a downlight in the vestibule of the room is actually the addition of perhaps 300 downlights throughout the hotel and potential cause for a rethink when the bottom line is bowing. However, because the room is central to the guest's stay, there is a strong case for its reconsideration.

'The concern should be to make people feel good, feel comfortable, to flatter them,' says Nathan Thompson of The Flaming Beacon. 'Rooms are always very difficult because normally one light has got to do three or four jobs pretty well. It's nice to get a good brightness modulation so there's no blandness anywhere, to play with accent.'

Hoteliers have been aware for some time of the shortcomings of room lighting and even in traditional hotels it is becoming a more considered area. On a practical level, additional facilities such as nightlights are being introduced so that trips to the bathroom are less disorientating and less disruptive to partners. Also with partners in mind, reading lights are being re-examined so that late night browsers of books or business papers cause no disturbance from over bright bedside lighting. With low-voltage tungsten halogen often too hot a source for the purpose, the solution is increasingly the expensive but effective fibre optics which provide a cool-to-the-touch fitting and tightly focused beam.

While few hotels are likely to emulate Ian Schrager's St Martins Lane (see page 106) by allowing guests to change the colour of their room with an interactive lighting system, some form of control would be an improvement and where it has been introduced has inspired positive feedback from guests. 'It adds a level of sophistication and sexiness that a couple of switches on the wall don't have,' says Jonathan Speirs.

In fact switching generally is one of the ripest areas for improvement as anyone will testify who has sat in bed late at night puzzling over how to switch off that one rogue light.

'One of the key things is the logic of where switches are, even in a typical room,' says Speirs. 'It takes you a few minutes to work out what each switch does and most times it's very illogical. Or there's the situation where you have to put your hand up inside the shade and fumble around – the lamp could be hot – to switch it on or off. The aim should be to make life easy for people – by the time they get to the hotel they want to relax a bit. A lot of hotel chains are addressing this area but the best solution has not been found yet.'

St Martins Lane, London, UK. COURTESY OF ISOMETRIX. PHOTOGRAPH © TODD EBERLE.

Penthouse, Metropolitan Hotel, London, UK. COURTESY OF UNITED DESIGNERS.

The Tides, Miami, USA. COURTESY OF COLUMBUS COMMUNICATIONS. PHOTOGRAPH © COOKIE KINKEAD (ISLAND OCTOPUS).

Bathrooms: washing with light

'Low-voltage downlights have arrived like a wave,' says Maurice Brill. 'For a long time operators wouldn't even consider them because they thought the maintenance factor outweighed everything, but they do provide an incredibly efficient means of light in an area where the guest is becoming more and more demanding.'

'The low-voltage light source is the best one to use because it makes a bathroom look more glamorous, gives it a sparkle that the old compact never did,' agrees Sally Storey.

Equally indisputably the mirror is the main focus. To produce a flattering result with no harsh shadowing on the features, the best approach is to side-light the mirror so that it provides a softer light to the face, supported by carefully positioned downlighting – not directly overhead and not so that glare will be produced by it reflecting in the mirror. A downlight could also be positioned over the shower. 'I think it looks like a dark hole without it,' says Storey.

If few rooms currently have dimmer switches, even less bathrooms feature them. However, they are yet another refinement in the St Martins Lane in London where a simple dimmer controls two Starck-designed Flos pendant lights over the basin. 'There are two scenarios,' says Gary Campbell of Isometrix which designed the scheme, 'one for when you're putting make-up on or shaving and need a brighter light and then a subdued light for when you are just pottering or relaxing in the bath.'

It may be even more worthy of consideration in those instances where low voltage has been embraced a little too enthusiastically. 'Some operators are putting enormous emphasis on the bathroom to the point where some of them have got far too bright,' says Brill.

The Grand, Brighton, UK. COURTESY OF MAURICE BRILL LIGHTING DESIGN. PHOTOGRAPH BY MALCOLM RUSSELL.

The Ballroom, Hyatt Carlton Tower, London, UK. COURTESY OF HYATT CARLTON TOWER. PHOTOGRAPH BY KEN KIRKWOOD.

The Ballroom, Hyatt Carlton Tower, London, UK. COURTESY OF HYATT CARLTON TOWER. PHOTOGRAPH BY KEN KIRKWOOD.

Ballrooms/function rooms: light fantastic

Corporate conferences and presentations, social occasions, fundraising balls, fashion shows – all these events represent a significant chunk of hotel turnover. The growth in this type of business coupled with the increasing demands of technology means that function spaces must be ever more flexible and sophisticated in lighting terms.

'There are technical advances all the time and demand in function rooms and ballrooms is growing constantly, so we're all becoming more educated as time goes on,' says Maurice Brill. 'A number of years ago it was regarded as being sufficient if you had chandeliers and wall brackets on a dimmer. Then along came the use of projection, the need to light stages and dance floors, the need to highlight tabletops and so on.'

Most complex is the ballroom. Whereas a function room is usually effectively a shell with the flexibility to suit a range of requirements, the ballroom has the added decorative element. 'A ballroom has got a major amount of lighting in it,' says Brill. 'Normally it would have recessed downlights, coffer lighting, function lighting, it may have chandeliers and wall brackets, it may have uplighting, it will certainly have a stage lighting facility. And it may with all of that still have fibre optics, which are a complete exercise in their own right.'

The ceiling is clearly the busiest area. In addition to recessed downlighting there will be perhaps cold cathode for the coffers (often two colours or even three in the case of the hotel which wanted to match companies' corporate colours). Chandeliers while not obligatory are ubiquitous and some form of large decorative focal element is helpful in terms of both scale and glamour. In refurbishments, existing traditional-style crystal chandeliers are commonly augmented with low-voltage lamps for more punch and sparkle.

An increasing emphasis on table dressing could mean track or low-voltage monopoints to allow highlighting of individual tables – with enough points to allow the reconfiguration of tables for different events. Track can be concealed in mouldings so it can't be seen from below or a mechanical arm system with a number of hanging points and sockets can be pulled down when needed. The arrangement of all fittings will also have to take into account possible partitioning of the space. It is essential that all of them are individually addressable by a lighting control system, the key to complete versatility of the space.

'The flexibility and variability of scenes and looks in these spaces is becoming accepted as very important,' says Jonathan Speirs. 'It's difficult if you're trying to keep the ceiling as clean and minimal as possible because that's where you've got to put all the stuff. You also need enough budget to give you flexibility. The combination of those two things could reduce what could actually be achieved.'

It is probably impossible to overstate the importance of lighting in this context. 'There is increased competition in this area,' says Speirs. 'Why would someone use your banqueting facility rather than go to the guy across the road? What is its USP that will make a difference? The room. What memorable thing can you design into the room that will make people come back? This is where the lighting plays a huge part.'

According to Nick Hoggett of DPA, conservatism and a reliance on traditional formulas has meant that lighting is still not fully exploited in this context. 'Lighting designers should be looking to encourage interior designers for more imaginative solutions – 95 per cent of the ballrooms you go into have either got coffered ceilings with cold cathode in them or traditional chandeliers hanging in the coffers. There's a great opportunity here to push the boundaries out and create interesting decorative elements.'

Grand Ballroom Foyer, Grand Hyatt Hong Kong, Hong Kong. COURTESY OF HANCOCK COMMUNICATIONS.

The Salisbury Room, Hyatt Carlton Tower, London, UK. COURTESY OF HYATT CARLTON TOWER. PHOTOGRAPH BY KEN KIRKWOOD.

Water Garden, Hyatt Carlton Tower, London, UK. COURTESY OF HYATT CARLTON TOWER. PHOTOGRAPH BY KEN KIRKWOOD.

Meeting rooms/business centres: conferring atmosphere

While they may veer from the grand to the bland, meeting rooms form an important part of hotel incomes. 'Lighting is often quoted as an important factor because a lot of them are dingy places – some of them don't even have daylight because they're tucked away – so the artificial lighting becomes really significant,' maintains Nick Hoggett.

Flexibility and ease of control are still the keywords in smaller corporate areas because of factors such as AV usage, but meeting rooms especially are likely to be used for long stretches and comfort must be combined with practical considerations. 'You want an environment that works for people to sit in for eight or ten hours. It's got to be pleasant but it's got to be workmanlike as well,' says Hoggett.

'We would generally approach it by having two or three layers to the lighting so if there is an all-day nuts and bolts meeting where people are pondering documentation there is a simple functional lighting scheme, perhaps embellished with some wallwashing or wall lights, for instance. Then perhaps there's another layer of lighting – some tungsten components that can be brought in over lunch or dinner.'

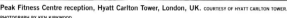

Peak Fitness Centre reception, Hyatt Carlton Tower, London, UK. COURTESY OF HYATT CARLTON TOWER. PHOTOGRAPH BY KEN KIRKWOOD.

One Aldwych, London, UK. COURTESY OF ONE ALDWYCH. PHOTOGRAPH BY KEN KIRKWOOD.

Fitness facilities: healthy glow

What began as a trickle in the '80s became a flood in the '90s resulting in the complete health complex that is now *de rigueur* in any deluxe hotel. The range of facilities and activities that can now constitute the health and fitness area – swimming pool, gym, sauna, steam room, cold plunges, massage, beauty salon – requires an equally diverse range of lighting treatments.

While many operators are still opting for fresh daylight colour temperatures, elsewhere, even in areas like the gym, trends are moving away from clinical brightness and towards a more textured approach. Indirect fluorescent (avoiding glare on TV monitors) to lift the ceiling area and provide ambient light might be complemented by a degree of wallwashing (possibly colour) and low-voltage highlighting for warmth and visual interest. 'One of the nice things about gym equipment is all the metal which allows you to create a bit of sparkle,' says Sally Storey.

'In the gym you hardly need any ambient light for safety because it's all done on screen,' says Maurice Brill. 'You need enough background light to set up the machinery, the rest of it can be a theatrical backdrop. So we accent some pieces of equipment and we try to insert some background colour with colour washing or projection.'

Pools, where light levels are not so critical, are becoming less municipal and more moody. Using the pool itself to locate ambient lighting is an aesthetically effective approach and one which avoids reflective glare from downlighting over the pool where lamp replacement also becomes an issue. Fittings used outside the pool will need to be IP-rated for the damp environment.

In treatment rooms, two of the primary considerations will be the type of source and its location. Tungsten halogen is the most flattering to flesh tones – and after all, this is an environment where people especially need to look good. Given that this is

also an area where people spend a lot of time on their backs, the overuse of downlighting should be avoided because of glare problems.

A lighting control system is once again essential, allowing a more upbeat scene in the morning, mellowing to a more relaxed mood in the evening. If a space has more than one purpose it will also mean that the ambience can be adjusted according to the activity.

'We've been approaching health and fitness like a bit of a place to explore, a bit of an adventure,' says Maurice Brill. 'Because everything else is so formulated, this is one area that doesn't need to be. It needs to be safe and you need to get the light levels where you need them. But they are quite interesting envelopes – you have machines in one, TV monitors in another, the swimming pool, the juice bars – and they lend themselves to lots of different methods of approach.'

Heathrow Hilton, UK. COURTESY OF DPA LIGHTING CONSULTANTS. PHOTOGRAPH
© NICK HOGGETT.

**The Emperor's Tower, Caesar's Palace, Las Vegas,
USA.** COURTESY OF ROSS DE ALESSI LIGHTING DESIGN. PHOTOGRAPH
BY PETER MALINOWSKI.

Peninsula, Hong Kong. COURTESY OF LIGHT DIRECTIONS LTD.

Exterior: outside broadcast

The general manager of a famous London hotel once expressed his concern to a lighting designer that the exterior lighting scheme, while attractive, was clearly an extravagance. The designer concerned informed the general manager that the cost of lighting the hotel façade each night roughly equated to that of a large gin and tonic in his own bar. The exterior lighting stayed on.

Non-existent or even inadequate lighting can negate any effort that has been expended on the interior. An effective scheme proclaims the hotel's presence and its image, it exudes a welcome message to the guest and invests the building with glamour. It creates a landmark.

It is also functional. 'I'm quite strong on the focus of the entrance so that you can immediately say where the entrance is,' says Sally Storey. 'From a distance you want to light the high level, but as soon as you approach the building you want to create the impact on the ground floor level so that you know immediately where to go.'

The increase of outdoor facilities has brought renewed emphasis on both exterior and landscape lighting. 'Traditionally the lighting designer was employed for the interior,' says Nick Hoggett. 'More and more we're being appointed for the interior, the architectural lighting and the landscape lighting.' While there is virtually no hotel that does not benefit from lighting the landscape – even if it's just topiary in a tub – the degree to which it is important is partly dependent on how much the landscaping is part of the facilities. In other words, resort hotels will be at the top of the scale in this regard.

Although there is huge scope for the flamboyant and exotic, a sense of mystery, an illusion of depth can be created by not lighting the whole thing up like a Christmas tree. Pools of darkness (as long as they are not unsafe or threatening) can be as lyrical as pools of light. And as lighting designers such as

Car parks: the light approach

Nathan Thompson of The Flaming Beacon have demonstrated, in tropical areas where pitch darkness is a natural state after nightfall, the stars can be as effective as any artificial pyrotechnics.

To have a grand front entrance to the hotel and grubby access from the car park rather defeats the object. 'What you don't want is a stinky dirty old staircase with a few emergency lights stuck on the wall,' says Nick Hoggett. 'Whatever form of pedestrian access there is between the car park and the hotel it must be smart at the car park end as well as the hotel end – lighting plays a significant part in that.'

A more sophisticated approach does not necessarily imply hi-tech or high costs. Painted coffers and the combination of linear fluorescent for the parking area and warmer temperature compact fluorescent (in more attractive fittings) to delineate pedestrian routes will produce a lighter, cleaner, smarter solution. A lift lobby with glass-blocked walls could have coloured backlighting using fluorescent – a simple but striking effect. 'It's a question of identifying lighting opportunities to make the car park a little less utilitarian,' says Hoggett.

Children's pool, Tel Aviv Hilton, Tel Aviv (top left, overleaf). COURTESY OF DPA LIGHTING
CONSULTANTS. PHOTOGRAPH © NICK HOGGETT.
Amanusa, Bali (bottom left, overleaf). COURTESY OF NATHAN THOMPSON/THE FLAMING BEACON.
Le Touessrok, Mauritius (right, overleaf). COURTESY OF ROSS DE ALESSI LIGHTING DESIGN.
PHOTOGRAPH BY ROSS DE ALESSI.

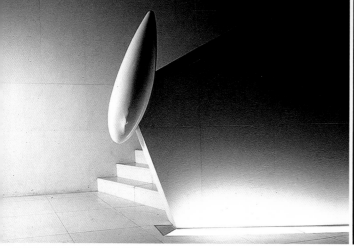

Staircase and lobby, Asahi, Tokyo, Japan. COURTESY OF PHILIPPE STARCK.

The Legian, Bali. COURTESY OF GHM. PHOTOGRAPH BY JUG BROWN.

General considerations: sources

The hotel environment is about people – what makes them look good and feel good. While energy saving is becoming more of an issue, there are still very few roles for discharge sources front of house. The colour rendering of compact fluorescent lamps has improved enormously in recent years, but like metal halide, quartz or ceramic, the coolness of the source makes it less than ideal in many hotel applications. The difficulty with dimming discharge lamps is also a huge disadvantage.

Tungsten halogen, both mains and low voltage, is still the most widely specified source. Despite being the most inefficient of all, GLS lamps are also still used in some cases. The crisp, white light of low-voltage dichroics is ideal for both ambient and accent lighting (the beam control possible with low-voltage fittings makes them the optimum solution for highlighting decorative elements such as sculptures or floral arrangements). When dimmed it becomes increasingly similar to candlelight, warm and flattering to skin tones.

'It's all down to how people look,' says Jonathan Speirs. 'You want to use colour temperatures that flatter people. You are talking about more incandescent or low voltage, with maybe very slight coloured filters to temper the crispness and sharpness – that depends on the style and image of the hotel. I think people have an expectation that when they walk into a period piece it's more incandescent and when they walk into a contemporary place it's more crisp white light.'

Lamp type also plays a role in establishing the market position of the hotel. 'If you have an inexpensive hotel you don't necessarily want to make it look expensive because you'll have people going away from the door,' says Speirs. 'Whereas if the expensive ones look too cheap and nasty people are also going to be deterred. A lot of sparkle and unshielded sources in a cheaper hotel may convey that impression or image, whereas that solution in a five star, high-end hotel is completely unacceptable because there will be more beautiful objects to look at rather than lots of sparkly, glittery, glaring lights.'

There is also the question of geographical context, though in hotels this seems to be less pronounced than, say, retail environments. In Asian shopping centres, for instance, it is common to find fluorescent sources at daylight temperature – a psychological refuge from heat and humidity. The association of tungsten halogen with glamour and luxury still prevails in urban hotels, however. In resorts, the preference is for even warmer sources.

'Resort style hotels in Indonesia, Thailand and Malaysia are seldom served well with raw tungsten halogen sources such as the ubiquitous MR16,' says Michael Huggins of Light Directions Ltd. 'The warm colours, woods, fabric and plants generally need softer, warmer light in these settings. Clever use of simple lighting solutions using Par 38 and GLS lamps produces excellent results. Adaptations of age old lighting solutions such as inverted ceramic pots, lanterns and even candles – enhanced for safety and effectiveness – also go a long way.'

Oulton Hall, Leeds, UK. COURTESY OF MAURICE BRILL LIGHTING DESIGN. PHOTOGRAPH BY MALCOLM RUSSELL.

Oulton Hall, Leeds, UK. COURTESY OF MAURICE BRILL LIGHTING DESIGN. PHOTOGRAPH BY MALCOLM RUSSELL.

General considerations: maintenance

No general manager is going to appreciate having to stock an enormous range of different lamps because every fitting in the place has its own peculiarity. Clearly some sort of cohesion is necessary in the sources specified throughout the hotel. 'We set ourselves an internal target of the maximum number of lamp variables and we do our best by revisiting the design and re-specing features,' says Jonathan Speirs.

However, a hotel is not a utilitarian proposition and there has to be a trade off in creating a visually textured environment. 'One of the biggest mistakes that is made in lighting in these areas is that somebody will use one downlight everywhere,' says Maurice Brill.

The same considerations apply to lamp life. Here economy is not the only factor, but also access. Longer life sources are more practical for high ceilings, for instance. Where access is particularly difficult – for certain exterior applications such as decorative canopy lighting, for example – fibre optics could be a better solution. Throughout the hotel, control systems will not only save electricity but also enhance lamp life.

A further issue is preserving the integrity of the scheme. The maintenance person up a ladder is rarely concerned or even aware that an exact beam angle might be somewhat crucial to the success of a concept. Aluminium rather than dichroic reflectors or fittings that lock into position are ways of countering subsequent indifference.

However, maintaining perfection is impossible and Nick Hoggett advocates that hotels adopt a policy of allowing the lighting designer to revisit the scheme on an annual or biennial basis to preserve its integrity.

'Although hotels are very good at their housekeeping, inevitably you have a lot of adjustable lighting and things don't get looked after exactly as they should. I think it would be good if we started a regime like a health check so the lighting designer had a long term relationship with the hotel.'

31

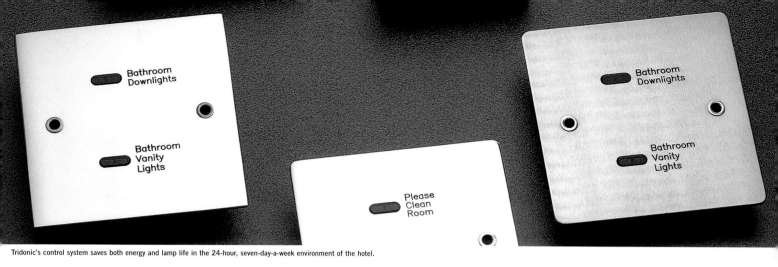

Tridonic's control system saves both energy and lamp life in the 24-hour, seven-day-a-week environment of the hotel.

Lighting control systems

The control system is a vital component in the hotel and leading operators have been using them for some 20 or 30 years. In this 24-hour, seven-day-a-week environment the lighting control system not only saves energy and lamp life (the life of low-voltage tungsten halogen lamps can be doubled when connected to dimmers; quality dimmers can extend that to five times normal life), but allows the lighting in key areas such as the lobby and guest room corridors to complement the time of day. On an aesthetic level it is the ultimate instrument for composing and fine tuning ambience.

In the corridors it is a matter of judicious dimming to create the appropriate light levels for the time of day and to conserve energy. In restaurants it is essential to conjure up a suitable atmosphere for breakfast, lunch and dinner scenes or for particular occasions. Brighter conditions suggest a more business-like scene that will deter people from lingering, while the dimmed-down evening setting will put diners in a more relaxed mood.

But of all spaces, the ballroom and function areas are probably the most complex and demanding in this regard. The control system is essential for their versatility and flexibility. It is the magic wand which helps transform the scene from business symposium to extravagant ball.

Lighting controls: considerations for ballrooms
It is important that next to each entrance door there should be a control panel for the lighting system, as this is the point of entry into the room. Furthermore, it is quite common that for functions a theatrical set may be erected along one wall, so obscuring access to one of the panels in that area.
• Within each space there should be a programming point (PP) to enable the reconfiguration or programming of part or all of the system while some areas are occupied. This allows personnel to programme the lighting without the need for long trailing cables.

• Due to the highly flexible nature of the space, one of the two control panels within a zone should be a touch screen controller. This provides maximum flexibility to the hotel staff and users alike, while offering a simple-to-understand graphical user interface. It should be possible to program hidden pages into the touch screen, so that only authorised users have access.

• The system should be provided with automatic room-join functions. These would take the form of magnetic proximity switches, mounted on the de-mountable partition tracks. These units would sense the current status of the partitions and then configure the local control panels to suit the current status. It must not be possible for someone operating a control panel in one space to be able to plunge the people in the next room into darkness. This would mean that with all of the partitions closed, each control panel would only control the lighting within that space. However, if a partition were to be opened between two rooms, then each of the local control panels would control all of the lighting within the enlarged space. The panels would then work in parallel. Similarly, if all the partitions were open, all local control panels would work in parallel and control all of the lighting.

• Another advantage of the touch screen controller is that in the unlikely event of the magnetic proximity switches failing, a function can be provided within the engineering pages of the touch screen to override the partition status. This is also useful if one of the partitions is only partially withdrawn – say, to form a buffet area during conferences. Access to the engineering pages would only be gained with the appropriate code being entered into the touch screen.

• Other typical pages would be a screen with a touch to raise, and re-touch to lower function. This is particularly useful where there are several large chandeliers. For special events it would be possible to set the intensity of individual chandeliers within the ballroom from this screen. Simply by

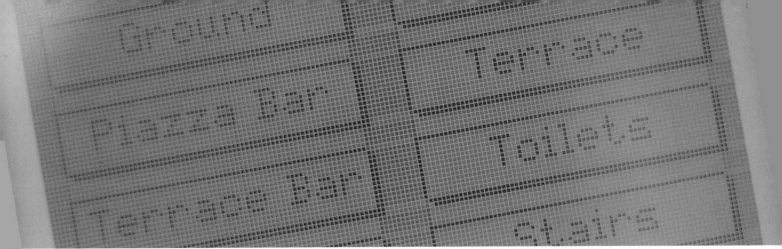

Under control: setting the scene for different times of day or evening is relatively simple using a touch screen display. COURTESY OF DYNALITE LTD. PHOTOGRAPH BY KEITH LOVEGROVE.

touching and holding a particular chandelier as shown graphically on the screen, the intensity can be slowly raised; as soon as the finger is removed, fading ceases. Normally, this would be a temporary setting and would not affect what was set in the dimmer's memory. However, a save function could be added to this page so that the new setting could be stored in the appropriate scene.

• Another useful screen can be created for the engineering department featuring practical functions such as lamp check, scene reprogramme and set-up. Special event scenes should also be made available

• Another type of control panel in a pre-function area might provide four pre-programmed scenes. These would typically be: welcome, cocktails and display, with the fourth scene being reserved for specially programmed one-off events. It could also be provided with a master fade-up and -down set of buttons.

• If they are on public display, control panels installed in the ballroom itself should be fitted with a key locking switch to inhibit their use. However, if they are to be installed behind lockable panels, then there is no need for the key switches. The panel may not have an off button, as a number of local authorities will not grant an entertainment licence to hotels where it is possible for the public to gain access to a control panel that could turn off all of the normal lighting, irrespective of the fact that there is emergency and maintained lighting.

• These ballroom control panels might be fitted with six scene selection buttons and a master raise and lower pair of buttons. Typical scenes might be: welcome, banquet, banquet cabaret, dining with dancing, wedding speeches and audio visual. The last would be used when there is slide or video projection on to a roll-down screen. Here it is vital that no light falls on to the projection screen and that the lights are dimmed down to an appropriate level to enable the best-possible picture visibility, while at the same time maintaining sufficient illumination for the audience to take

notes.

• A further panel could be installed in the service corridor. Unlike the smart panels detailed above, this would be a configurable control panel, with a dedicated operational programme installed in its on-board processor. It can serve two functions; first, as the only means of turning off all of the lighting in both pre-function and ballroom areas. This off-scene would have a slow fade, to give any personnel in the area time to leave before the lights turn off completely. This is a very important function, as the cost of leaving the lights on for periods when the room is not in use, both from an energy consumption point of view (lighting load and air conditioning) and reduced lamp life, are considerable. Second, the 'on' function would provide a cleaners' scene. It is again important that this provides enough light to enable the cleaners to perform their duties efficiently without wasting energy. Equally, cleaners are notorious for forgetting to turn lights off.

• A further consideration is wireless remote control for conference scenarios, for use by presenters who are using slide and video projection. It is also a useful tool for the hotel sales manager, who will regularly need to show prospective clients around the ballroom. He or she can walk around the space and demonstrate several standard lighting scenes to the prospective client, without the need to be distracted by having to use local control panels or the touch screens.

(Source: David Kerr, Dynalite, manufacturers of architectural dimmers and building control systems)

projec

section two

Coconut lanterns glowing in deep tropical darkness and candles glimmering behind sculpted ice; sky beams grazing the Las Vegas cityscape and rooms reverberating in rainbow colours. From the simple to the sophisticated, from function to fantasy, from understated to over the top, lighting in hotels explores the full spectrum of sources and techniques. The following case studies demonstrate that there is no such thing as a typical lighting scheme in this environment, but equally that lighting is crucial to the hotel experience from the moment guests sign in at reception to the moment they turn out their bedside lamp.

The Point Hotel, Edinburgh, Scotland
Lighting design: Jonathan Speirs and Associates
Architect and owner: Andrew Doolan

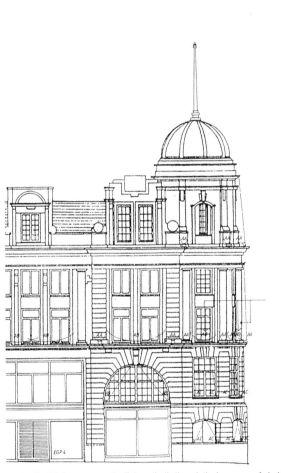

PHOTOGRAPH © PAUL ZANRE

The interior lighting announces itself dramatically through the large areas of glazing (right).

Such is the prevalence of incandescent sources in leisure environments that the use of fluorescent lamps is more likely to say hostel than hotel. But part of the current rehabilitation of the source is evidenced in its application in more prestigious venues such as The Point. With the right treatment, it becomes dynamic and different, not downbeat and downmarket.

The redevelopment of the 1914 classically designed building, formerly a large store, has won both architectural and lighting design awards. The concept was to develop a contemporary interior for the existing building – and to allow it to announce itself dramatically when viewed through the large areas of glazing that had constituted the shop windows of the store.

'When guests arrive by lift they are greeted
Only when they step out into the lobby is it

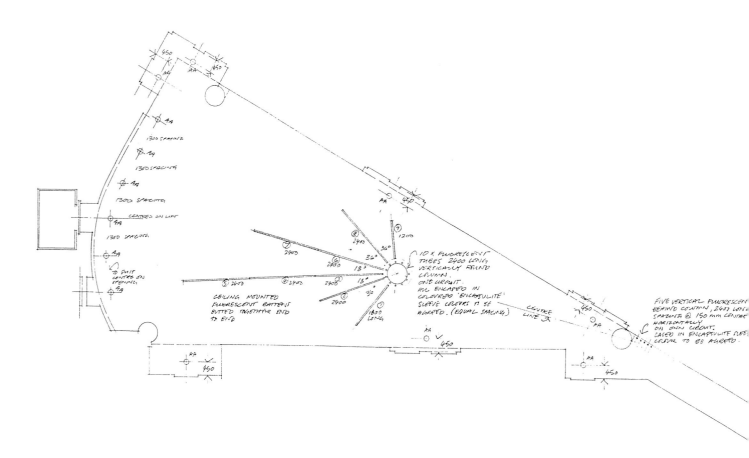

Lighting had to be integral to that concept. The brief also had to consider extremely limited finances and that future maintenance of the scheme was crucial to the success of the project. None of these factors was considered a constraint in creative terms, however. 'Our aim was to inject something memorable and colourful into the scheme,' says JSA's Gavin Fraser.

The inspiration behind the radical concept for the triangular lobby spaces on each floor was Dan Flavin's fluorescent light sculptures. In addition to recessed downlighting above each guest room door, simple Fitzgerald fluorescent battens with Encapsulite colour gel sleeves were wall mounted to create a solution that was both cheap and chic.

Each floor level is characterised by particular colours. The batteries of battens are located either behind existing large white plaster columns or wall reveals, so that when guests arrive by lift they are greeted with walls painted in striking colours. Only when the guest steps out into the lobbies is it apparent how the effect is achieved. Looking back towards the lifts the batteries become a considered part of the architectural composition.

with walls painted in striking colours. apparent how the effect is achieved.'

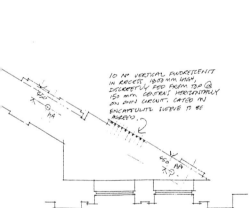

Using fluorescent battens with different gels, each floor level is characterised by different colours.

Some were also positioned so that they could be viewed from outside through large semi-circular windows. 'Because of its simplicity the scheme allows for changes of colour to be made every few months or so without spending great amounts of money – dramatically changing the appearance of the interior lobby spaces and the exterior façades,' says Fraser.

In order to emphasise the contrast between the classical sandstone façade and the new contemporary interior, the exterior treatment uses Meyer metal halide floods and spots located on shelves and ledges to produce a simple, restrained white light scheme.

'The triangular plan, the vast empty space and the use of coloured washes of light for optimum effect serve to illustrate how lighting, when well considered, can lend drama and excitement to a space that has been reduced to its simplest architectural elements.'

Arctic Hall, Jukkasjarvi, Swedish Lapland
Lighting designer: Kai Piippo
Original architect: Aimo Raisanen

By backlighting the corridors from the outside (facing page) **Kai Piippo adds to the magic: 'just the effect of light and the structure itself'. The sea-themed suite** (overleaf), **like the other suites, is designed and lit individually.**

'The light at once brings the ice alive yet, in the form of heat, threatens its existence.'

Few lighting assignments can be as ephemeral or extraordinary as a hotel which literally melts away each summer. Arctic Hall, 80 miles north of the Arctic Circle, sleeps 120 people and has a restaurant, church, cinema and art gallery. It is rebuilt every year entirely from ice, cut from the frozen surface of the River Torne. In the winter, temperatures at the 1,200-square-metre complex can fall to minus 30 degrees Celsius, occasionally dropping to minus 47.

The effects of light on such a translucent substance as ice are ethereal and powerful. There is a paradox, however. The light at once brings the ice alive yet, in the form of heat, threatens its existence. 'It is the most interesting project that I have been involved with so far,' says Kai Piippo. 'My idea was to play with the contrasts between light and dark, and cold and warm colour temperatures. I also wanted to create a magical world with no equipment visible – just the effect of light and the structure itself.'

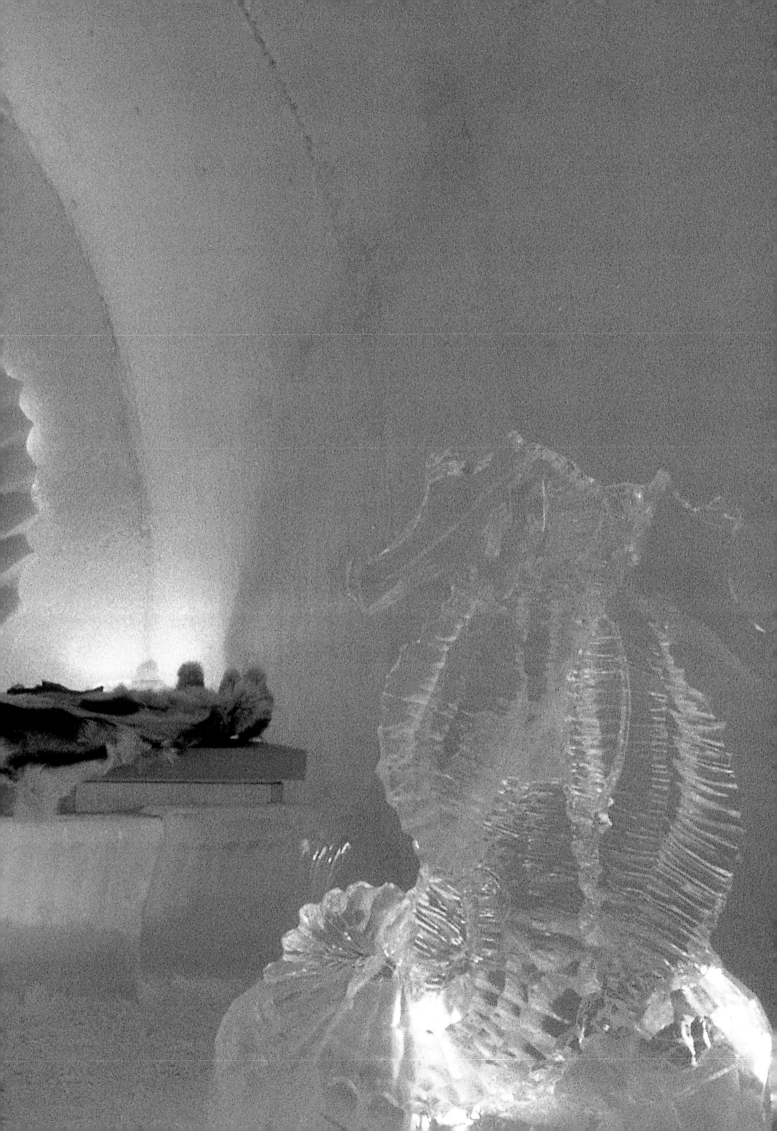

To create a contrast between light and dark, the corridors are left unlit – the only sources of illumination are backlit ice walls (using exterior fittings) and spill light from the rooms and suites. The rooms themselves, completely furnished in ice and minus three degrees Celsius, are lit simply with an 18W fluorescent tube with 'warm' filter located under the ice bed. 'We could use very little light but still get the wanted effect,' says Piippo.

The lesson of how much lighting to use has been learned from the hotel's first incarnation. Many of the fittings were badly positioned and threw a lot of their heat forward. An ice sculpture was destroyed by a low-voltage spotlight placed too close. Insufficient insulation on other wall-mounted fittings contributed to the internal melting of the walls. But less is often more, agrees co-owner of Arctic Hall Oke Larsson. 'Because of the reflectance of the ice blocks, you don't need powerful light if you put it in the right place.'

Sources have also been carefully selected. In the columned hall, the chandelier is illuminated using fibre optics to give multiple cool light points from a single 50W tungsten halogen lamp. The light box is located on the roof so the heat rises. Also on the roof are the two 18W fluorescent fittings, with blue filters, which provide internal illumination for the top of the pillars in the bar. These are supplemented with candles on the tables, while the rest of the ambient light again comes from backlighting the walls from outside. A technique used throughout, where the bars and corridors are concerned, it is achieved with We-ef 70W metal halide floods with blue filters. In the chapel the sole lighting comes from three exterior 100W Bega tungsten halogen floods, two with blue filters. 'A contrast between warm and cold was used in the way that all the ice inside the hotel was to shine cold while the warm light which comes from the rooms gives the private space a cosy feeling,' says Piippo.

The lighting of the suites, each of which has a different designer, varies according to the scheme. Fibre optics are used for some of the ice sculptures and furniture. In the sea-themed suite, two 18W fluorescent tubes with lavender and blue filters respectively are positioned under the bed, while a tungsten halogen strip light with blue filter backlights the scallop-shell bedhead. In the 'Birth of the Ice' suite, recessed ultraviolet tubes add warm purple tones to the predominant blues. Throughout, strategically positioned oil lamps or candles lend their warmer colour temperatures to a bedside table or ice carving. In the long winter with little or no daylight, the artificial lighting is crucial. 'The idea was to create light so that it felt like daylight,' says Piippo.

'Fifty per cent of architecture is a question of how to use the light,' says original architect Aimo Raisanen. 'Especially in the Arctic area where we have just a couple of hours of daylight between December and January, much can be done with the right lighting.'

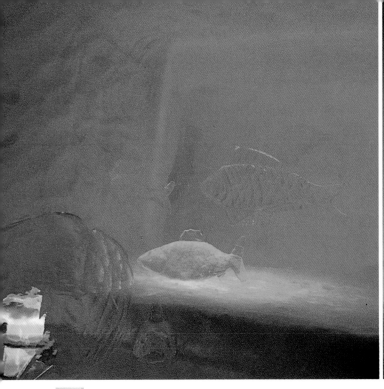

Playing on cold and warm colour temperatures: throughout cool public space contrasts with cosy private space.

Grand Harbour Hotel, Southampton, UK
Lighting designer: Maurice Brill Lighting Design
Architect: Igal Yawetz and Associates

PHOTOGRAPH © TONY HARRIS

The Winter Garden viewed from the outside acts as a beacon (facing). Low-voltage striplight in the lobby ceiling coffers is switched up in the day to balance the brightness of adjacent glazed areas (above).

'Downlights pick up the square patterns on the flooring to create alternate accent and shadow.'

With a busy main road to one side feeding the ferry terminal and the town, and a significant stretch of waterfront to the other (housing overspill from the annual boat show), the Grand Harbour is in an optimum position to attract attention. The aim of lighting designer Maurice Brill was to leave that in no doubt. 'The object of the exercise was to advertise the hotel,' says Brill. To achieve that, the main element he concentrated on was the striking pyramid structure known as the Winter Garden, two of its sides solid and the third, the waterside frontage, fully glazed. 'A lot of people use the road and at night their first view of Southampton is the Winter Garden,' adds Brill. 'I wanted to generate something that was a bit different.'

Inside the Winter Garden, guests experience a series of atmospheres (facing page). **At the entrance, under-run tungsten halogen uplights pick up the gold of the sign while blue flourescent lamps illuminate the glass pyramid** (above left). **Pool lighting** (above right and overleaf, far right) **fades from white to mellow blue in the evening.**

Brill also felt that the lighting scheme could help characterise an area which had a nebulous function as a tea room-come-lounge. 'We wanted to generate a unique space for the hotel because the Winter Garden didn't have any portfolio attached to it – it was a space to have tea in the afternoon and take your drink into in the evening. We had the opportunity of doing something really quite architectural.'

The starting point was the idea of transforming the space on a daily basis so that guests staying more than one night would experience a series of atmospheres. Theatrical techniques were employed with a range of pre-programmed Source 4 colour projectors. Equipped with leaf pattern gobos, some were positioned at a very high level to project on to and colour wash the walls, and others were positioned slightly lower to hit the floor. These were supplemented below by a bar of low-voltage, very narrow beam AR111 spots highlighting the planting and the tables. Other recessed low-voltage lighting washes the floor. All spots were very tightly focused so that no light hits the glass to cause glare or mask the view.

The treatment extended to the exterior, but was restricted to the pinnacle of the pyramid. (Elsewhere on the main body of the building 150W narrow beam metal halide fittings in the ground and on the façade itself, graze light between the windows). At high level on an adjoining roof, 400W MB1F blue projectors create a startling blue apex. 'There is virtually no exterior lighting here except one or two bollards to depict the edge of the water,' says Brill. 'The water is deliberately not lit to act as a mirror image.'

Colour, on a simplified scale, was also used to switch moods in the pool area. Column-mounted dish uplighters feature two low-voltage sources under two differently coloured segments of glass, one white, one blue. White is used during the day to generate a bright, healthy 'workout' feel. This slowly fades to blue in the evening to create a quieter, more soothing ambience. The approach also resolves the problem of extensive glazing at one end of the pool. 'I wanted to drop the night levels significantly so you didn't feel as though you

Clikstrip at knee level round the counter front and simple low-voltage downlighting create a warm, intimate space in the fish restaurant (facing, above). The bar is warmed even further with 150W GLS lamps combined with tungsten halogen (facing, below).

were in a goldfish bowl,' says Brill.

This creation of alternate atmospheres is a prevalent theme throughout the hotel. While the overriding intention was to create warm, intimate spaces – the exterior lighting was kept cool to emphasise that intimacy – demarcation of different venues was also a key strategy. The bar, for example, unusually breaks the tungsten halogen rule with 150W GLS lamps for its ambient lighting to increase the cosiness and softness of that space and to increase the contrast with adjacent areas such as the Winter Garden, brasserie and lobby.

The lobby, around which the other spaces are arranged like the spokes of a wheel, is altogether whiter and brighter. Cold cathode in the ceiling coffers is combined with very narrow beam low-voltage lighting to accent the columns and pinspot the floral arrangement on the central table. In between the cold cathode a series of 50W low-voltage downlights pick up the square patterns on the flooring to create alternate accent and shadow all the way round. 'What I call footsteps of light,' says Brill. 'I often use this technique to pull people round spaces.' Wide, frosted downlights in a ceiling trough round the perimeter give an even wash on to the walls. During the day the cold cathode is switched right up to avoid too much contrast between the lobby space, which is naturally relatively dark, and the brightness of the adjacent glazed areas. In the evening it fades down to produce a softer effect with a strong accent on the floor and the centre.

The brasserie, by contrast, is flooded with natural light during the day, but by night is a more challenging space to subdue. A high ceiling is just one factor which militates against a sense of intimacy. It also raised a maintenance issue in that lamp replacement would be difficult. Both problems were resolved with recessed 250W Par 38 lamps for the ambient downlighting, simultaneously providing a good lamp life and a warm source. Decorative incandescent fittings were mounted lower down on the columns to create a local ambience. The space was further warmed with tungsten halogen Clikstrip on top of etched glass screens and 100W double focus low-voltage lighting directed to the Roman blinds which shield the glazing.

Even more problematic was the ballroom. The ceiling void, though almost two metres, was restrictive for the amount of services to be pulled through – 'Architects just aren't appreciating how much of a void is needed above the ceiling,' comments Brill – and the distance between the coffers made it a difficult engineering job. In pure lighting terms, it was also a challenge to produce any punch. Downlights around the coffers are the principal light source, while 50W narrow beam low-voltage lamps were inserted into the crystal chandeliers alongside the existing GLS sources to increase the sparkle. 'It was also to get some impact on the floor where I was struggling to get any real accent light. Although we had achieved a good ambient light we needed highlight as well,' says Brill. To increase the glamour factor, the whole module was dropped, and blue and white cold cathode inserted allowing colour switching between the two.

Hilton Hotel, Durban, South Africa
Lighting designer: Maurice Brill Lighting Design
Interior designer: Khuan Chew, KCA Intl.

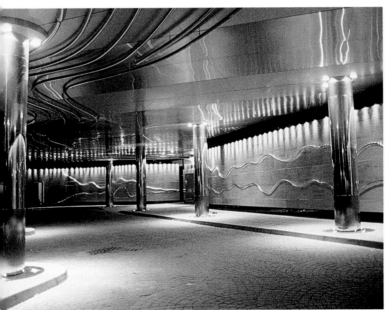

Drama and vibrancy are the keynotes in the lobby (facing page), *porte-cochère* (above left) **and glass stairway to the first floor** (above right).

'White light punches up through the water to the stairs bathing them in a subtle glow.'

The brief for this particular incarnation of the international Hilton chain was straightforward and to the point. 'They wanted something that had a lot of vitality and drama,' says Maurice Brill. 'Khuan likes colour and theatricality.'

Where the cavernous lobby was concerned, drama was less of a problem than vitality. 'It's such a huge space that we were worried it would end up feeling like a banking hall,' says Brill. Several strategies were adopted to warm the space. First, low-voltage fittings were used at the top of the smaller columns to graze the marble with fingers of light. In the high ceiling, clusters of narrow angle 250W Par 38 downlights (whose long lamp life helps maintenance) both illustrate the architecture and highlight the central floor area. 'The idea was to impact the floor area so you give it a definite heart – there is a central brighter axial point to the lobby,' says Brill.

Rivets, a bar with dance floor area, is a dynamic blend of sources and techniques (above and facing page, top and bottom). **Blue cold cathode brings out the cool qualities of steel on an exterior terrace** (left).

White glass discs with mirror backing are brought to light with fibre optics for a contemporary take on the traditional chandelier (above and facing).

Cold cathode concealed in coving at second floor height breaks the verticality of the space, while scallop wallwashing (also Par 38s) and low-voltage in-ground uplighting for the central sculpture niche add further softening. Uplighting was also cleverly used for the glass stairway which leads to the first floor. At ground level a water feature is used to locate 300W submersible low-voltage luminaires. The white light punches up through the water to the stairs bathing them in a subtle glow.

In the lift lobby, drama was increased by a predominance of uplighting rather than downlighting, which is restricted to highlighting the central floor area. Low-voltage 50W burial fittings are located either side of the lift doors throwing theatrical pools of light on to the ceiling.

A feature of Rivets, a bar with a dance floor area, was two full-height curved glass screens with a 'wave' pattern etched into the glass. Each wall is made up of two pieces of glass, and in between are four 300W water ripple projectors creating the gentle motion of light bouncing off a water surface which spills out across the ceiling. This creates a calming inner sanctuary within this exciting bar. The curved blue glass behind the bar is backlit top and bottom using 20W low-voltage fittings. Elsewhere a variety of sources and techniques are combined to bring dynamism to the space: low-voltage fittings are recessed into the bar canopy while 100W mains voltage fittings provide uplighting above; Clikstrip on the bar front creates a warm glow to the floor and in front of that a row of fibre optics delineates the divide between the hard floor and the carpet; low-voltage uplighting to the columns picks out the eponymous rivet detail.

In a hotel where vibrancy and theatricality is the brief, the ballroom is no place to fight shy of the possibilities. Rather than resorting to the time-honoured crystal stand-by, Khuan Chew designed a contemporary version of the chandelier using a series of white glass discs with bevelled edges and a mirror backing at ceiling level. Here fibre optics are used to give sparkle within the ceiling line. A series of fibre optic tails also lead into each layer of glass. The spectacular results are effected by pre-programmed projectors with colour wheels. Elsewhere materials such as stainless steel need only a simple treatment to bring out their dramatic potential. For an exterior terrace, where it was used extensively including for the ceiling, the approach was to backlight with blue cold cathode.

For the *porte-cochère* where again it features heavily in columns, walls and ceiling, metal halide exploits the cool mirror effect of the steel columns with four 70W downlights positioned around the top. Although these were planned as uplights – 'They couldn't get them in so we turned them the other way round,' says Brill – the result is still distinctive. The line of Par 38s used to downlight the walls in a series of elongated scallops starts before the canopy to lead people up the sweeping drive. 'Throughout it was a question of treating each area individually,' says Brill, 'but the brief was always keep it lively, bright, sharp and dramatic.'

Hotel Adlon, Berlin, Germany
Lighting designer: Licht Kunst Licht
Architect: Patzschke, Klotz and Partner/AIC

PHOTOGRAPH © ERCO

The colour of the standard mounting ring was matched throughout, from plain pool-side setting (facing page) to frescoed ceiling (top).

'The main aim was to find one system which could answer all the questions.'

Such a complex proposition as a hotel invariably demands an amalgam of different lighting techniques and technologies, according to the varying requirements of each space. This clearly has implications for maintenance and, where expert input has not been used to rationalise this to some degree, it can result in a hotel stocking an almost infinite variety of lamp types for replacement purposes. At the Hotel Adlon this rationalisation was taken to its most logical conclusion – the development of just one basic low-voltage luminaire type, designed by LKL (Licht Kunst Licht) and manufactured by Erco, for the ambient lighting. With a diameter of just 125mm and a light aperture of 40mm, it features one standard mounting ring and was evolved largely to meet the demands of an extremely tight construction schedule.

'The hotel was assembled like a ship – everything was pre-made in Italy and then assembled in Berlin,' says LKL's Andreas Shulz. 'The uniform diameter of the ring meant they could be built into the ceilings at an early stage. This enabled the installation of all luminaires at a later date after completion of all the finishing works. There was a variety of different ceilings, some fresco, some

The effects from a single fitting varied from pinspotting in the American Bar (above), punching down on to the lobby floor (facing above) to scalloping on the main stairway (facing below).
PHOTOGRAPH COURTESY OF HOTEL ADLON (above and facing).

highly decorated stucco, and the colour of the light rings was adjusted accordingly.'

Just one type of lamp – low-voltage tungsten halogen with pin base and from 35W–75W – was used for cost management and maintenance reasons. 'One of the biggest problems in lighting design in hotels is very different fittings, very different lamps and very different transformers,' says Shulz. 'We also have just one type of electronic transformer which can handle everything from 20W to 75W. We have 9,000 transformers, but they are all the same.'

The specification of an aluminium reflector rather than a cool beam lamp was also to avoid a further maintenance issue – that of ensuring the integrity of the lighting scheme. 'We didn't use cool beam lamps because the beam angle can be changed later. Everything was static – the reflectors were static so you just change the lamp. Our lighting scheme was guaranteed. This is a big problem because maintenance is always cheap and those people are not interested in our lighting design ideas.'

While the outward appearance of the fitting is uniform throughout the hotel – it was installed in rooms and suites as well as public areas – it has been adapted to meet the requirements of those diverse areas. Possibilities range from downlights with beam angles from five to 40 degrees, pivotal directional fittings with a swivel angle of up to 30 degrees, and direct/indirect fittings for the soft lighting of ceiling coffers. 'We have around 15 effects – different kinds of wallwashers, different holes in metal plates which cover the fittings and so on,' says Shulz. 'The main aim was to find one system – using light in a concealed way, making it as unobtrusive as possible – which could answer all the different questions.'

Amanpulo, The Philippines
Lighting designer: The Flaming Beacon
Architect and interior designer:
Francisco Mañosa and Partners

PHOTOGRAPH © GEOFF LUNG

Festoon lighting in an upward facing timber box is typical of the low-tech, local material approach (facing page). The restaurant ceiling was lowered to allow more effective pinspotting of the basket display (above).

Hotels such as Amanpulo take people's conception of what a tropical paradise should be and attempt to turn it into reality. The sanitised version of the local vernacular, it is irresistible as everyone's ideal of the get-away-from-it-all experience without getting too far away from life's luxuries.

That sense of escape was a central part of the lighting strategy with its high contrast, dramatic light patterns. 'The way we wanted it to be was nearly too contrasty and nearly too dark and nearly too edgy,' explains Nathan Thompson of The Flaming Beacon. 'This is about trying to make things a little bit unreal. It's about trying to forget a little more easily about whatever you're getting away from when you decide to go to this hotel. When you walk through the front door it's not quite like a theatre set but it's somehow unreal.'

The approach is also about the integration of light and architecture, concealing sources wherever possible. 'The general strategy with this kind of project is to avoid light being in your face and trying not to give it any identity. It's very anonymous, purely there in a reinforcing role.' Occasionally, in such a simple structure, that involves a degree of ingenuity. In the bar lounge, for example, part of the general reception area, the challenge was to uplight part of the timber-panelled ceiling unobtrusively. The solution lay in the metre-high tube-shaped lamps which were positioned on the bar at the far end. In addition to the GLS lamps which provide a general glow, a concealed Par 38 lamp sits at the top to provide the upward component.

PHOTOGRAPH © NATHAN THOMPSON/THE FLAMING BEACON

High-contrast levels are sustained in the retail outlet (above) **and the library** (previous page), **with low ambient lighting and sharp pinspotting.**

Elsewhere in the space, the pilasters are picked out simply with downlighting using wall-mounted timber boxes (again with Par 38s) with additional GLS downlighting in between. The timber boxes occur throughout the project, typically to express the verticality of columns, and epitomise the low-tech, local material approach to the lighting. 'We tried to choose materials that were appropriate to the degree of technology inherent in the space we were working in,' says Thompson. 'It would have been most inappropriate to use fancy high-pressure die-cast aluminium German or Japanese fixtures in a place where most of the craftsmanship is about using cane and finely crafted wood. There's nothing wrong with making a little box out of wood and sticking a bulb up inside it.'

Incandescent sources are used throughout, typically in the beach club where GLS sources enclosed in festoon strips are concealed within an upward facing timber box to spill light on to the lower struts of the roof. 'This is a very simple detail which we achieved by tight co-ordination with the architect-designer,' says Thompson.

Even the 'Philinea', an incandescent tubular lamp which can only be found in the more obscure recesses of the Philips catalogue, is used to create a flattering glow in capiz shell diffusers either side of dressing tables in the rooms. Its energy consumption prohibits its widespread use, however. For the display cabinet in the 'library', a T8 tube (2,700K, colour rendering R80 plus) substitutes as concealed downlighting. 'We have used Philinea at the vanities because the colour is better on the face, but the power is pretty crazy. If we'd used Philineas at the display cabinets we'd have ended up with cabinets which use more power than the local houses.'

'high-pressure die-cast aluminium fixtures
about using cane and finely crafted wood.'

PHOTOGRAPH © NATHAN THOMPSON/THE FLAMING BEACON

A concession is made to an energy-greedy incandescent tubular lamp to give a warm, highly flattering glow through capiz shell diffusers (above).

In the restaurant the scheme is based on low-voltage accent lighting. Such was the level of co-operation between designer and lighting designer that it was agreed the ceiling should be lowered to enable more effective pinspotting of the series of baskets displayed in a zigzag wall arrangement. In addition, small MR16 fittings with gobos project leaf patterns on the ceiling – 'there was some planting which had lighting in the base and it seemed appropriate to pretend that some of those shadows were falling on the ceiling' – while narrow beam MR16 fittings pinspot perimeter tables. A more general approach was taken to downlighting in the central area where tables were liable to be moved, thus making precision pinspotting impossible. 'It seems to work well to have a pinspot-per-table strategy in one part of the room where tables are in a fixed position and to leave a zone that the operator's happy with in the centre.'

Throughout the hotel high contrasts are created by the interplay of general and accent lighting, the colour temperatures of which were manipulated using a sophisticated Dynalite dimming system (the hi-tech element is behind the scenes). 'Generally we were using low-voltage for accents and GLS to provide a colour background level,' says Thompson. 'For general lighting I like to have wattages way too high then turn them right down, and for accent lighting put wattages too low and turn them all the way up. So the colour contrast is very clear – a very warm general light, but a whiter, crisper accent.' Both prompted by and responding to the architectural environment, the lighting scheme is both simple and sympathetic. 'It's motivated primarily by the architecture – it's plain and trying to be clear,' says Thompson, '...at the same time it's trying to help the architecture.' And the same goes for Thompson as it does for the guest: 'It's not just about escapism, but immersing yourself in the place you are.'

Balina Serai, Candi Dasa, Bali, Indonesia
Lighting designer: The Flaming Beacon
Architect/interior designer:
Kerry Hill Architects

PHOTOGRAPH © RIO HELMI

Exterior circulation areas have minimal lighting (facing page, above and overleaf) – **enough to navigate by while retaining the sense of complete tropical darkness.**

'In places, the scheme is as much about what hasn't been lit as what has.'

Like Amanpulo (see page 62), Balina Serai is in the paradise resort market, but as a three-star hotel it is pitched at a slightly less affluent Eden seeker. While the same lighting principles applied – heavily attuned to the architecture and again concerned with creating high contrasts – the scheme is subtly different as a result. 'There's a little more concern about utility here,' says Nathan Thompson of The Flaming Beacon. 'The concern is still to create the right brightness patterns and complement the architecture, but it was a question of working a little bit harder to make sure that lighting works on a task level as well. In that sense, the Balina Serai is more real.'

Positioning an R63 fitting at the top of the roof supports complements the architecture while providing task lighting to the balcony (above).

While the lighting of vertical elements was a keystone of the strategy at Amanpulo, the Balinese structure allows this aspect to be exploited to an even greater extent. With most Balinese buildings of this type being open structures, the lack of walls means an emphasis on the columns for the positioning of fixtures. 'You just illuminate the vertical rhythmic stuff, the rows and rows of columns,' says Thompson. 'With these kind of structures the columns can be close together so you can get some very dramatic rhythms, more so than in Amanpulo where the building grid is much wider. It's lighting reinforcing the architectural concept.'

The technique is evident in the open corridor which approaches the lobby. Timber downlights with R63 sources are positioned at the top of the square plaster columns. Opposite, on the rough stone wall a series of simple plates made from attractively grained wood, with two golf ball lamps behind, are set some 80mm off the surface, grazing light both up and down the wall. The light pattern on the wall echoes the rhythm of the columns opposite. 'We are trying to make the light represent the two different elements – the columns and the wall,' says Thompson. 'The wall lights are also useful because they drop light where you want it – they provide circulation light so you can find your feet – but they also get a pattern of accents on the wall.'

The same dual function is achieved with the lighting of the balconies. 'This was a question of choosing the position of the lights well so they do something for the architecture, but at the same time provide the kind of task lighting required so that people could read, for example.' On the top level an R63 fitting at the apex of the roof supports fulfils these twin objectives, while avoiding glare to guests on the balcony. On the lower level, located between the columns is the timber plate wall light.

Like the balconies, lighting in the corridors exploits the vertical rhythms of the structure (above).

In the reception, tight beams – 'as narrow as I could get them' – streak down the columns from Par 38s and R63 lamps. As with Amanpulo, simple contextual materials are used for the fittings throughout – a square timber box for square columns and a round cylinder made from coconut wood for round columns. 'If you cut coconut wood the right way and use the hard timber which is round the outside you get these beautiful, delicate grained structures in the timber. We played with that to create shells to house downlight.'

The illuminance on the columns is doubly effective where they are adjacent to water. The temptation to light the water itself has been resisted with a more restful and effective result. 'We felt this was an appropriate way to deal with reflecting planes – light things which you can see reflected in them,' says Thompson. 'Some places try to light inside the pond and you can see the mud on the bottom and things swimming around, but it doesn't tell you anything about the slippery reflective nature of the top of the water surface which is much more interesting.'

In places, the scheme is as much about what hasn't been lit as what has. To guests from First World countries inured to street and amenity lighting, Bali is a dark place where night falls swiftly with little preamble. The aim was therefore to reflect this in the lighting approach. Exterior circulation corridors have minimal lighting – a staircase, a garden pot – enough to navigate by without inducing a sense of artificiality. 'You want to see the stars,' says Thompson. 'It doesn't matter if you can't see the beautiful scenery at night, you can see the beautiful scenery in the daytime. There is a possibility to reinterpret it at night, leave a lot of stuff out of the picture. It's a good reason not to put too much light in.'

Hotel Kempinski, Munich, Germany
Lighting design: Francis Krahe and Associates
Architect: Murphy/Jahn Architects

PHOTOGRAPH © KEMPINSKI HOTEL AIRPORT

Metal halide uplights the cool, spacious atrium canopy and is also used for the intersecting floor-based stripes of light at the centre of the project (facing). Projected coloured light patterns in the airport/hotel link provide a vibrant welcome (above).

'Bold, colourful patterns of light help guests to find their way around.'

Appropriately enough for a hotel attached to an airport (the 400-room Kempinski was the first phase of a commercial service zone at Munich's recently built airport), navigation is a major theme of the lighting design. 'Bold, colourful patterns of light help guests to find their way around and make it a more interesting place to visit,' says Francis Krahe.

That light journey begins in the pedestrian tunnel which links the airport to the hotel. Here the cool and warm colour temperatures of metal halide and high-pressure sodium lamps are combined with colour filters to project coloured light on to white walls. These are viewed through perforated metal screens. As well as providing a vibrant welcome to night-time arrivals, the resulting contrasts and colour patterns distort perception of the tunnel's size.

The hotel entry from the walkway tunnel (above) and the beer garden (facing) have a consistently geometric theme.

The cool spaciousness of the entrance atrium is complemented with metal halide uplighting to the canopy (400W floods and 1,000W spotlights). Soft blue filters on some fittings emphasise the triangular pattern of the roof structure. The blue tints evoke an early evening sky while the unfiltered white light allows changes in colour and intensity for different events and times of day.

The transparent, crystalline quality of the atrium structure is further enhanced by the illumination of key glass elements: a series of two-metre-square glass fountains which are backlit with fluorescent; the glass floors of the lifts and stairs (uplit with fluorescent pendants); and shattered glass frames which are accented with dimmable roof-mounted halogen fittings.

The geometry behind the scheme – 'Lighting fixtures arranged in bold geometric forms are used to overlay a pattern of light on the architecture and landscaping,' says Francis Krahe – finds its most literal expression in the two intersecting floor-based stripes of light at the centre of the project. Each 750 feet long, they are embedded in the paving of the hotel driveway. One blue, one yellow, they are formed by light pipe under frosted glass and lit by 250W metal halide lamps with coloured lenses. The yellow line extends to form a yellow edge to the parterre garden while the blue line separates the bar from the public circulation area. The judges who gave the project a Citation in the International Association of Lighting Designers awards called it 'ephemeral, fantastical – an exciting and unusual hotel environment'.

Metropolitan Hotel, London, UK
Interior and lighting design: United Designers
Architects: Mark Pinney and Associates

The internally lit Perspex rods which surround the DJ's booth in the Met Bar are one of three elements which stand out against the dimmed down low-voltage downlighting (facing).

'We wanted to have some glamour in there. The glass tables and chocolate brown Venetian polished plaster bounce the light round a lot.'

The Metropolitan Hotel is a designer hotel and it is uncompromising in the clientele it is aiming at – professionals involved in the four Ms, namely: the media, modelling, movies and music. 'The customer profile for the Metropolitan bears more relation to attitude and lifestyle,' says Keith Hobbs, who together with partner Linzi Coppick created the interior scheme. 'This was typically translated into a target group that could be termed "young spirited".'

In Nobu restaurant (top), top lighting using concealed fibre optics results in glowing glass panels.

In the lobby the ambient lighting is punctuated by the pinspotting of decorative objects (above), including a bas-relief clock (right).

A special three-tiered system was designed for the bedhead in guest rooms (facing).

In the Met Bar, materials and the way they interact with light were a primary consideration (above).

The project was also seen as a tripartite concept – a contemporary hotel, a trendy New York-inspired restaurant and a happening late night private members bar. 'All were destined to attract the style-conscious and all three were to have independent entrances, different and distinct styles and, although adjoining, be essentially separate operations,' says Hobbs.

In line with its cool understated approach, the lighting is simple. This is not an environment where the lighting scheme could afford to be overtly spectacular or showy. However, this has not precluded the imaginative or even the innovative.

Ambient lighting throughout is dimmable low-voltage downlighting by the Light Corporation. In the lobby this is punctuated by the spotlighting of decorative objects, including a dramatic bas-relief clock, to provide visual contrast. A piece of etched glass inset into the timber and leather reception desk is illuminated from beneath by a 50W low-voltage spot. This shines upward to light a clear glass vase and floral arrangement above. 'Our philosophy is to incorporate lighting into our designs and we often hide lights within furniture and fittings to make architectural and design features lit, but not in an obvious way,' says Linzi Coppick.

This same discreet effect is achieved in Nobu restaurant with its South American-influenced Japanese cuisine. Here rows of oblique floor-to-ceiling etched glass panels divide the service route from the customer area and provide the space with its most striking feature. The panels are recessed into the ceiling where, hidden from view, they are lit from the top using fibre optics. While the same glowing effect could be achieved with cheaper fluorescent sources, the space within the ceiling was too confined. 'However, using fibre optics meant that we had a neater detail at the top of the glass because we didn't have to have an access panel to change the lamps,' says Coppick.

In the Met Bar there are three main lit areas which stand out against the dimmable low-voltage downlighting. A mural is uplit, in a somewhat

unorthodox manner, with low-voltage downlights turned upside down and positioned behind a banquette. The bottles behind the bar sit on an opal glass shelf illuminated with fluorescent lighting for a backlit display. The third component is the DJ booth which is surrounded by, initially, glass and then by less destructible clear Perspex rods, lit internally using fluorescent tubes at the base. 'At night it's dark and you can just see these patches of light – the mural, the bar and the glow of the DJ booth,' says Coppick.

In an environment that had to run 24 hours, from breakfast sittings to late night sessions, the materials and the way they interacted with light were an important factor, according to Coppick. 'We wanted to have some glamour in there. The glass tables and use of the chocolate brown Venetian polished plaster bounces the light round a lot, particularly for the breakfast and lunch sessions when you are trying to get more effect.'

The guest rooms, designated by fluorescent backlit amber glass squares, were given considerably more attention in lighting terms than the average hotel. In addition to low-voltage downlighting, wardrobe lighting and dressing table luminaires which complement the main bedside fitting, the headboard was specially designed to take a three-tiered system. A conventional looking lamp with an incandescent source is for more general lighting; attached to the bottom of it, through a shelf, is a reading light with flexible arm and small 10W halogen lamp; below that, a nightlight panel with a thin striplight enables easier navigation to the bathroom in the night.

'It was very important to us to get a good level of light for reading – we knew of no hotel at the time that had a decent reading light so that you could read in bed without disturbing your partner, while a nightlight means you don't feel you are in an alien environment,' explains Coppick.

'It was also important to create a general romantic light – to create a good ambience and a feeling of well-being in the room. It's taking what's available but making it work in an even better way.'

St Davids Hotel, Cardiff, Wales
Lighting designer: Olga Polizzi/Concord Lighting
Architect: Patrick Davies

Exterior and interior lighting exploit the drama of the structure (facing, above left and right).

St Davids is Cardiff's – and the principality's – first five-star hotel. Designed by Patrick Davies for Rocco Forte's new RF hotel empire, the hi-tech structure with its soaring bat-wing roof sits on the edge of Cardiff Bay. The lighting strategy was to maximise the drama of the structure, both inside and out.

Key to the project is the atrium, a minimal space with monolithic walls rising up a vertiginous 36 metres. The high degree of daylight, the unrelenting whiteness and a desire to preserve the purity of the space with no visual clutter such as luminaires added up to a considerable challenge in terms of the lighting.

'We found it very hard to do because there were so many hard surfaces and it was very, very white,' says Olga Polizzi, design director of RF Hotels. 'You've got nowhere really to put any lighting.'

'Blue-glassed floods and elongation beam projectors light the façade, fusing with the white interior lighting for a spectacular frontage.'

Metal halide fittings uplight the floating bat wing (above). Roof-mounted projectors provide interior illumination of the atrium (above right). Specially designed fittings snake off the wall to downlight the reception desk (facing).

The primary solution was to illuminate the atrium from above. Bega 250W metal halide projectors were mounted on three-metre poles on the glass roof where they shine down into the space below. Also on the roof, Bega 400W metal halide floods and projectors uplight the floating bat-wing structure.

Inside the atrium, the lower ceiling above the lifts was an opportune space for recessed low-voltage spots (Torus 100). Without disrupting the clean curve of the atrium balcony, these highlight the artwork, which helps to lead visitors towards the lifts. The reception was a further problem area. 'We've got no back of reception, we've got no top of reception, so it was jolly hard again to know how to light it,' says Olga Polizzi.

Eventually luminaires were specially designed and made by Concord Lighting, who supplied the majority of fittings on the project. The serpent-like fittings cantilever off the atrium wall, downlighting the reception desk with Hi-Spot mains-voltage halogen lamps. While lacking the punch and sparkle of low-voltage halogen they have the advantage of needing no transformer. Low-voltage dichroic downlights in the corridors add a twinkle and a further layer of light to the atrium space. To continue a subtle nautical theme throughout the hotel, these are complemented by elements of blue on the columns (low voltage with blue halo diffusers) and following the curve of the lift wall, and in the blue backlighting of room numbers.

The exterior also picks up the light motif with Bega blue-glassed floods and elongation beam projectors (both 250W metal halide) lighting the façade, fusing with the white interior lighting for a spectacular frontage which shines out across the bay.

The Bonham Hotel, Edinburgh, Scotland
Lighting design: Jonathan Speirs and Associates
Architect: Ron Galloway Architects
Interior design: JSA and Janey Armstrong Interior Designs

PHOTOGRAPH © GAVIN FRASER

The giant lampshades are used to identify the building from the street during the day and at night-time.

'The shades add drama to the interior, while cocking a sly snook at a hackneyed hotel device.'

Condé Nast *Traveller* magazine named the Bonham as one of the world's coolest new hotels for the 21st century. A conversion of three grandiose terraced Victorian town houses, the hotel from the outset was to be 'dramatic, bold and stylish,' says Gavin Fraser of JSA.

The interiors juxtapose new and old elements together in a rich and eclectic manner, intended to be sympathetic to the old building while at the same time strikingly confident and modern. From an early stage, the idea developed of using lighting to identify the building from the street both by day and night.

The shades not only provide an ambient glow but also house five spotlights that can be used for accenting.

From outside, the façade comprises three two-storey bay windows, each of which became identified with the three main public activities in the hotel: reception, restaurant and conference.

Each of the windows was fitted with massive specially designed 1,200mm diameter hanging shades, thought to be the largest in Scotland. The shades have two lighting components. Standard frosted GLS E27 lamps are used in the centre to achieve an internal glow. In addition, five AR111 gimbal spotlights on suspended rings within the shade base add an accenting component for furniture or other elements below. Literally acting as a beacon, the shades also add drama to the interior, while cocking a sly snook at a hackneyed hotel device. 'Their dramatic scale plays with clichéd notions of the typical chichi table-light-in-window scenario often used by hotels in this context,' says Fraser. 'The Bonham shades take this notion to extreme and playfully offer an almost cartoon version of what we all recognise as a light.'

One Aldwych, London, UK
Lighting designer: Lighting Design Intl.
Architect: Jestico and Whiles
Designer: Mary Fox Linton

PHOTOGRAPH BY KEN KIRKWOOD (and overleaf)

Warm sources accentuate both architectural detail and a sense of welcome. The uplighting of the steel mesh can be glimpsed through the entrance (facing page). The pool (above) and health club reception (overleaf) use lighting to create peaceful and vibrant atmospheres respectively.

'Wherever you are in the building, you know you are in One Aldwych.'

One Aldwych is one of a crop of contemporary London hotels which are helping to confound the formula for international blandness and banality. Invariably mentioned in any conversation about designer hotels (and, like Edinburgh's Bonham – see page 88 – nominated by Condé Nast *Traveller* as one of the world's top 20), One Aldwych is the last word in understated sophistication. 'The brief was therefore to provide a lighting scheme as discreet as possible to reflect that understatement,' says LDI's Sally Storey. 'The idea was also to create an underlying ethos so that wherever you are in the building, you know that you are in One Aldwych.'

One of the most impressive features in the lobby/bar area is the double-height steel mesh wall which has been uplit using fibre optics set in the floor. The larger lenses used for a more intense effect in the higher volume space are stepped down in size as the wall turns the corner into a single-height space.

Tungsten halogen uplighting behind.banquettes and narrow beam dichroic uplighting of the columns helps reduce the sense of height in Axis restaurant (previous page). Fibre optics were used for discreet reading lamps in the guest rooms (above).

A five-metre high ceiling meant that maintenance was an issue. Soft ambient lighting is therefore provided by ceiling recessed 120V 250W Par 38 fittings: 'Because of their 6,000-hour lamp life,' says Storey, 'and they have a good even coverage which meant we could minimise on the number of fittings required.'

Elsewhere, lighting is used to create focal points – low-voltage uplighting to reveal the drama of the window arches; pinspotting (with AR111s) for the floral arrangements either side of the bar; and white cold cathode to light a brushed silver slot midway down the front of the reception desk, breaking the dark mass of the wood. Although table lamps had been planned into the original scheme, the interior designer decided to dispense with them. Their function was fulfilled with specially designed parchment wall lights which were originally positioned to provide a softer, indirect light compared with the downlighting and to bring the level of the space down. 'The wall lights became even more important as a way of bringing in a softer light beside the seating,' says Storey.

Another primary public space was Axis restaurant, which has its own front entrance with a flight of stairs leading downwards into a double-height and single-height basement area. Here, old, in the form of a renovated decorative lantern, is mixed with new in the fibre optics which are used to light individual stair treads. In the restaurant proper, the same issues that arose with the double-height lobby are also resolved with Par 38s for the ambient lighting. A coffer illuminated with warm xenon striplighting, and narrow beam dichroic uplighting of the columns, helps to reduce the sense of height and create intimacy. Linear tungsten halogen floods for uplighting behind the banquettes fulfil the same role.

While understatement is the keynote throughout, a degree of vibrancy is permitted at the entrance to the health club, where white

White cold cathode in the reception desk is one of several focal points in the lobby (above).

frosted glass on the front of the reception desk is backlit with blue neon. 'Reflecting into the curved wall opposite, it is a very pronounced effect,' says Storey.

The pool is typical of recent trends in this area of lighting. To avoid a sense of the municipal at all costs and create a more luxurious, atmospheric environment, Bega low-voltage tungsten halogen fittings are used to light inside the pool (their good coverage meant only four were necessary), while AR111 exterior fittings (Light Projects) positioned close to the walls create the most overt effect by imitating streaks of sunlight, leavening the basement space.

Perhaps the least understated architectural element at One Aldwych is the ornate Edwardian façade which afforded an ideal opportunity for light modelling. The warm stone suggested consistently warm sources – a mix of tungsten halogen and ceramic metal halide in the form of spots and floods located at various levels. 'We wanted it to be inviting,' says Storey.

The entrance is emphasised with specially designed floods which light the carvings above the door; AR111 in-ground uplighters which focus on the corbels, and Par 20 ceramic metal halide uplights to highlight the door reveals. The aim was also to pick out the main detail of the façade, the architrave moulding around the window, which involved positioning floodlights on the window balconies while countering a risk of spill light into the rooms. 'Locating the light sources on the window balconies is quite unusual for a hotel because of glare going into the bedroom windows,' says Storey, 'but by using spreader lenses and louvres, we could make sure the lighting just emphasised the architrave detail. The concept was to accentuate the architecture. It was an important, prominent site as it's the first thing you see as you come over Waterloo Bridge.'

Hotel Poluinya, Hokkaido, Japan
Lighting designer: Lighting Planners Association
Architect: Toyo Ito and Associates

The straight line of the two-storey guest wing (left and overleaf) pierces an oval space which extends from a bridge over a pond into the lobby (above).

'We treated the architecture itself as a lighting feature.'

While few designers welcome financial constraints, there are occasionally instances where in hindsight they become a virtue. At the Hotel Poluinya, a tight budget pared down the lighting solution to a simple yet stunning scheme with an unmistakably Japanese imprimatur. The key to its success is the high level of integration of the lighting with the architecture. 'By proposing the lighting design concept at a very early stage of the architectural design, we tried to integrate light into architectural details,' says Kaoru Mende. 'In other words, we treated the architecture itself as a lighting fixture instead of installing expensive fixtures.'

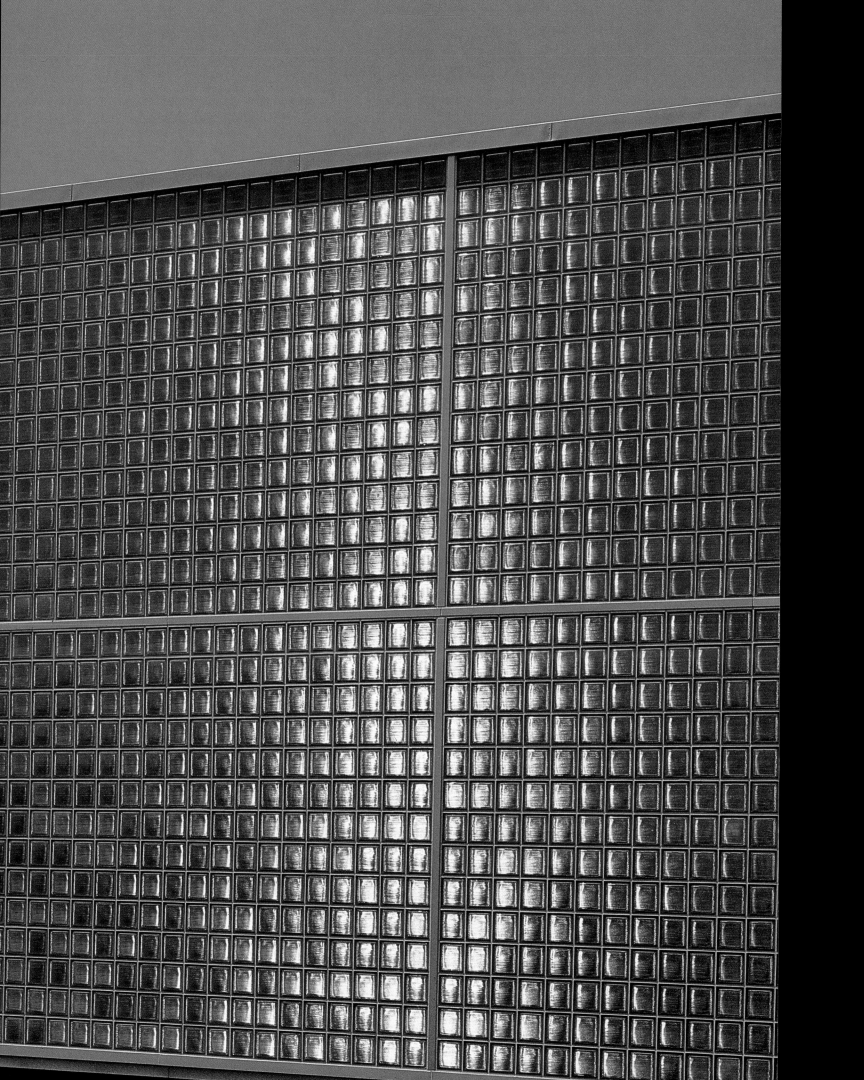

In the restaurant narrow beam low-voltage downlights provide pools of light (above). To illuminate the glass block wall, fluorescent sources, supplemented by MR16s, are concealed in vertical slits between ceiling and concrete wall (facing).

The hotel is small with just 26 guest rooms. The straight line of the two-storey wing pierces an oval public space comprising an entrance lobby, a multi-purpose conference hall and a restaurant/bar. The oval extends from a bridge over a pond into the lobby, courtyard, restaurant/bar and terrace. Each area is divided by four glass plates to give perspective and accentuate the depth of the oval and also to minimise the presence of light fittings. 'The lighting design attempted to symbolically visualise this clear cut plan by focusing on three themes – to present the straight glass wall as a landmark, to emphasise the transparency of the divided oval space, and to symbolise the entrance area filled with water,' explains Reiko Kasai of LPA.

The glass block wall delineating the passage that gives access to the guest rooms is indirectly lit with 26W fluorescent lamps, without fittings, placed in vertical 80mm wide slits between the ceiling and concrete wall. These are supplemented by 12V 20W low-voltage MR16 tungsten halogen lamps with mirrors. 'The glass block wall that takes in natural daylight turns into a glistening landmark at night,' says Kasai.

For the pool entrance area, specially designed fittings with 100W metal halide lamps were recessed into the wall. 'Reflections of shallow water in the entrance project ripples on the wall where symbolic encounters are intended,' says Kasai. 'Standing on the bridge one can enjoy the contrast between the curved wall in the light and the flat wall in shadow that suggests the stillness of a lake in the moonlight.'

Elsewhere basic 12V 55W low-voltage downlights provide both ambient lighting and, in narrow beam versions, pools of light in areas such as the restaurant.

'Good architectural lighting design can be achieved only with excellent architectural design,' says Kaoru Mende of LPA. 'For the Poluinya, excellent architectural design, the beauty of nature and darkness, and the extremely limited construction fee made it possible to enhance the quality of lighting design.'

St Martins Lane, London, UK
Lighting designer: Isometrix
Overall design: Philippe Starck
Production architect: Harper Mackay

PHOTOGRAPH © TODD EBERLE

In the Light Bar the double height voids are dramatised with saturated colour (facing). During the day its closed doors add a dynamic element to the lobby as a back projection screen for moving images such as swimming goldfish (above).

'A truly unforgettable visceral experience.'

Few hotels parade such PR hype as St Martins Lane – 'a new paradigm', 'a truly unforgettable visceral experience', 'magical and exciting, exuberant and fun' – but then few hotels are capable of living up to the hype. Like Morgans, Royalton and Paramount in New York, Delano in Miami Beach and Mondrian in Hollywood, this latest Ian Schrager hotel – and his first European venture – doesn't just boldly redefine the traditional concept of the hotel, it blasts it out of the water.

The conjunction of Shrager and Starck is now a celebrated one and at St Martins Lane has resulted in an idiosyncratic environment – 'truly stylish without being about a particular style', in PR parlance.

Lighting is a vital and intrinsic ingredient of the design concept – the tight co-operation between design teams is self-evident throughout the project – demanding a high level of customisation and an extraordinary attention to detail on the part of lighting designer Isometrix. Fittings were to be as discreet as possible and considerable consideration paid to their appearance. Downlighting was affected by Starck's stipulation that there should not be too many holes in the ceiling. Fluorescent and cold cathode were rejected on the grounds of light quality in favour of an almost completely tungsten/tungsten halogen solution.

ST MARTINS LANE **ASIA DE CUBA**

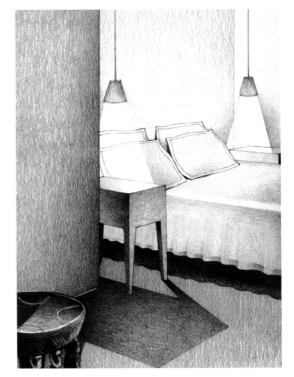

ST MARTINS LANE **GUESTROOM**

ST MARTINS LANE **LOBBY**

ST MARTINS LANE **LIGHT BAR**

In the lobby, ambient levels are kept low so *objets* can be zapped, with light for a gallery effect (previous pages). A colour change fitting within the bedhead allows guests to paint their room according to their mood (facing).

Penthouse suites are lit simply with Starck-designed Flos fittings.

Where overall strategy is concerned, the lobby epitomises the central ambition. 'The general concept was that a lot of the lighting should be concentrated at low level – it's more cosy, more atmospheric,' explains Gary Campbell of Isometrix. 'Starck also likes to have the ambient light levels really low and just pick out pieces of furniture or sculpture, to zap them with light so there's a bit of drama. The lobby is almost like a little gallery space.' Dimming is crucial here, as it is throughout the project – in each space in the lobby there are eight different pre-programmed scenes stepping down from very bright to virtually dark.

Specially made 35W low-voltage burial uplights (no flange, just a 3mm stainless steel edge with frosted glass diffuser) define the perimeter of the space with soft scallops and are used in clusters of four to graze the base of the six large columns. For the reception desk, made of stone enclosed with yellow glass, the symmetry of the scheme is retained but with fibre optic uplighting – with sources sandwiched between the stone and the glass, and thus inaccessible, they were the most practical option.

Balancing the lower perimeter lighting is a wash light set into a slot between wall and ceiling. A customised 50W low-voltage tungsten halogen fitting with spread-lenses achieves a greater warmth than fluorescent or cold cathode and more power than the other conventional choice of strip lighting. 'The cove lighting brought out the planes of the space,' says Campbell.

As highlighting was a key part of the strategy – the lobby is a setting for an eclectic mix of *objets*, from flea market finds and sculpture to Starck whimsy such as the gold 'molar teeth' stools – the challenge was to achieve it while minimising the number of downlights in the ceiling. The solution was a specially designed fitting which holds three or four dichroic lamps at once, all independently adjustable, so that several objects could be highlighted from a single ceiling aperture.

As a purely decorative effect, and using a similar technique formerly employed at Mondrian, three tungsten halogen theatre projectors concealed in the ceiling void create a narrow white light strip which slashes the lobby floor in an oblique line from the entrance to the restaurant.

PHOTOGRAPH © TODD EBERLE

The exterior lit effect is artfully produced by the dynamic colour change system in the guest rooms.

To one side of the lobby is the Light Bar whose acid-etched glass doors, closed during the day, act as a further dynamic element in the space. Using back projection, the doors double as a canvas, initially for a cross fading colour change system, and more recently with a DVD projector which allows more dramatic moving images – trees blowing in the wind, goldfish swimming in a bowl. At night the doors slide open and the projector is removed to reveal a dark space – black floor, grey walls – up to normal ceiling height. The drama comes from the four double-height ceiling voids, each painted a different colour (green, yellow, blue and orange/red) and each lit with a complementary colour to give an intense glow. Using the same technique as for the lobby cove lighting, the effect is produced by 50W tungsten halogen fittings with dichroic coloured glasses and spread-lenses.

'The problem we had with cold cathode, for instance, was throwing the light up,' says Campbell. 'We found we had to use reflector lamps in order to get the light right to the top of the void. It's actually quite high – two floors high. We needed something that was really going to punch the light up there, but that we could also dim.' The only other lighting element is the low-voltage pinspots which sidelight a display case of antique crystal glasses, so that it 'glows like a jewel' says Campbell.

Nowhere in the hotel has coloured light been used in a more revolutionary manner than in the guest rooms themselves, white box canvases which guests can paint according to their whim. Within the bedhead is a specially detailed colour change fitting (subject to a patent) based on a series of low-voltage tungsten halogen lamps with spread-lenses. With the aid of a simple dimmer switch this takes guests through a cross-fading spectrum of 100 colours – six saturated – allowing them to choose the shade they want, according to time of day, disposition or activity. 'The system produces a very even, intense wash of colour – it floods into the whole room and sets the mood,' says Campbell. Artfully, the system also takes care of the exterior lit effect, producing a series of jewel-like window sets, with an additional dynamic element whenever a guest changes the colour of a room. 'St Martins is purposely designed to have a high colour input so the colour forms a very strong part of most areas,' says Campbell. 'It's obviously designed to be very different from anything else in London. The emphasis is on looking at lighting in a different way, not looking for the obvious and on integrating the lighting into the architecture.'

The Palace of the Lost City,
Bophuthatswana, South Africa
Exterior lighting design: Ross De Alessi Lighting Design
Architect: Wimberly Allison Tong and Goo

PHOTOGRAPH © ROSS DE ALESSI LIGHTING DESIGN (and facing)

Vignetting the edges of the building to suggest a sense of history had to be balanced with conveying an atmosphere of warmth and welcome (facing and above).

'An idyllic archaeological remnant of a lost civilisation – a sort of *Indiana Jones* meets *Lost Horizon*.'

There are certain hotels – most notably in Las Vegas – that fall into the 'Disneyesque' category. Primarily resort hotels, they have moved beyond the mere business of accommodating people and into the realms of fantasy.

The 352-room Palace of the Lost City in Bophuthatswana, a two hour drive north west of Johannesburg, South Africa, is an extraordinary example. An oasis (literally, it is also a water park) in an isolated desert valley, the hotel has been invested with its own mythology. The concept was to suggest an idyllic archaeological remnant of a lost civilisation – a sort of *Indiana Jones* meets *Lost Horizon*.

The powerful animal sculptures which form a strong decorative element are primarily lit with tightly focused MR16 fittings.

The lighting plays a key role in establishing this illusion – even before the guest has set foot over the threshold. 'The central idea was to create the sense that the Palace was deeply rooted in the ancient culture of the surrounding locale,' explains Ross De Alessi. 'This translated, for example, into using the technique of vignetting the edges of the building – having them, via the lighting, seem to fade off, ghost-like, so it would look historical.'

It was also crucial that visitors should feel welcomed rather than spooked by this archaeological apparition. 'A lot of guests arrive in the middle of the night,' says De Alessi. 'As you approach the hotel a feeling that warmth and hospitality awaits you had to be conveyed. Even unoccupied towers and spaces were made to look lived in through lighting.'

The towers are the first feature to strike approaching guests. The tallest, the Kings Tower, is internally lit with a real flame torch within its main cupola. Low-voltage dichroic lamps (MR16s) were used to balance this effect visually with the other towers, which are illuminated solely by electric lighting. These each have four 300W quartz floods, dimmed down 60 per cent to simulate the colour of flame, which wash the patinaed copper palm frond roofs. The colour is supplemented with tinted compact fluorescent wall packs which also serve as safety lights.

The same floods are used to light the lower exterior walls of the towers, with asymmetric 120V 350W and 500W versions employed for the taller Kings Tower. 'The floodlight is positioned against the tower wall so that it bounces light off a reflector built into the balustrade and back on to the wall to create a soft glow rather than a harsh uplit look,' explains De Alessi. 'The deck behind the balustrade also glows and creates the illusion there's a burning brazier there, accompanied by guests enjoying the night air, even though those decks are really uninhabited.' Internal and external lighting to the towers is separately controlled to achieve balance between the two, and for dusk to night-time adjustment.

A three-tiered system is used for the Rotunda. The base is ringed with 1,500mm cool white fluorescent in lensed uplights to flatter the patina colour of the large leaves. The central section is lit by dimmed roof level Par 56 heads with snoots and louvres. Two 12V

five degree pinspots tightly focus on the finial. The lions are uplit with three lensed, snooted and louvred MR16 fittings.

Just in front of the Rotunda, the kudu (an antelope) fountain is illuminated with submersible, non-filtered MR16 fittings with linear spread-lenses producing a bright white effect. Waterproof spread-lensed MR16 fittings were again used for the gold-leafed cheetah fountain, this time with glass diffusion and colour filters, to provide sidelighting and uplighting of the dramatic sculptures. MR16 fittings, with lenses and snoots, are used to highlight most of the dynamic animal sculptures which form a strong decorative element throughout.

'With South Africa's 240V 50Hz line voltage, filament sizes of lamps must be quite large,' says De Alessi, 'so employing the 12V MR16 fixtures is a must for critical focus lighting, with their small filaments and great beam control.'

Elsewhere, Par lamps were specified widely – in submersible 300W Par 56 narrow spot versions to uplight the exterior of the lobby lounge area, for instance, and in burial and surface-mounted uplights (combinations of 80W, 120W and 150W quartz and incandescent Par 38s) to highlight tall columns.

Where most hotel projects are concerned, energy efficiency plays second fiddle to aesthetics in public areas. The desert location of The Palace of the Lost City, however, dictated that it move further up the list of priorities. 'In any design that I do, I always consider energy conservation,' says De Alessi. 'In this project, because it was located in the desert and because it was expensive to bring power out there, I used compact fluorescents wherever I could – for example, the bollards, the stairwells and the tower domes.'

A further constraint was preserving the fantasy – luminaires and cabling had to be kept strictly out of sight. 'The client insisted on having his building set aglow without visible fixtures. All cables are dressed and concealed within rock work. Tower panel uplights, for instance, are concealed in balustrades through tight co-ordination with the architect.'

MGM Grand, Las Vegas, USA
Lighting designer: Ross De Alessi Lighting Design
Architect: Klai::Juba
Designer: Dougall Design

The Gateway of Entertainment, a 170-foot diameter entry dome, is designed to recall the luminosity of art deco (facing and above). Recessed MR16 fittings uplight the bronzed bowls which also house 7KW oscillating sky beams (facing).

'The charge was to create a room evocative of another era.'

When the brief is to light the entrance to the world's largest hotel and casino, owned by a Hollywood entertainment giant, and when that hotel is in Las Vegas, the chances are that understatement is unlikely to enter the equation. However, for the art deco-style MGM Grand, there was a degree of subtlety required. 'The owners insisted that it compete with the surrounding glitz,' says Ross De Alessi, 'but not be "typically Vegas".'

Where the Lion Entry was concerned, the concept was to create a water and light ballet surrounding MGM's lion logo, manifested as the largest bronze sculpture in the world. The setting – fountains, columns, walls, screens and landscape – continues 300 feet north and 700 feet east from the site, one of the city's most prominent corners. A choreographed show continues across this 1,000-foot stage day and night, with LED screens on during the day.

The Lion Entry, featuring the MGM logo, is a complex water and light ballet where concealment of fittings was a key concern (previous page). The palm trees which form part of the landscaping were lit with narrow beam ceramic metal halide fittings (above).

The architectural and feature lighting comprises several elements: the lion statue itself, the fountain, architectural façade, screen frames, the large atlas bowls on top of the columns and landscaping. 'Visually besting the neighbouring competition with a high degree of colour and animation, yet staying within the deco-inspired theme by concealing luminaires within architecture and landscaping was paramount,' says De Alessi.

The lion was lit with dimmed Par 64 quartz and dichroic lensed metal halide from the front and sides to give it shape and dimension. These fittings were given artificial shutters as a theatrical reference. The sculpture is also lit at the bottom with dimmed quartz to warm the base and increase the illusion of height. The fountain – multi-tiered waterfalls and jets – was illuminated with multi-coloured submersible 250W and 500W quartz fittings of varying beam spreads and intensity. Separate circuits allow colour balancing and orchestration to music, saving energy and easing maintenance as only one third of the system is used at any one time. Pedestal jets are uplit only in white to harmonise with the lion's feature lighting.

The bronzed atlas bowls glow with recessed quartz 50W MR16 focal fittings concealed in the column and pilaster tops. To anchor them visually, the columns and pilasters themselves are uplit with concealed 35W and 70W ceramic metal halide fittings. The bowls also house 7KW oscillating sky beams which can be seen from all over the city. Special precautions were taken to ensure they caused no problem to air traffic at McCarren International Airport a mile away. The control system was programmed and physical stops installed to prevent more than a five degree tilt towards the airport.

Palm trees were uplit with very narrow beam 150W ceramic metal halide fittings located behind the screens, while the screen pilasters were also uplit with Par lamps. The lighting of the screen frames is orchestrated to complement the screen animation with concealed and dimmable neon (three colours plus white) to create a broad range of cross-fading or flashing colour. Another animated element is the cyclorama wall which runs the length of the project, lit with multi-coloured Par uplights and robotic fittings, 'a riot of ever changing and chasing colour.' Nevertheless the result is less 'Vegas' than the competition. 'Unlike the strong washes of bright light and exposed luminaires at other Las Vegas façades, MGM's Lion Entry is an exercise in restraint through concealment of smaller, efficient luminaires,' says De Alessi.

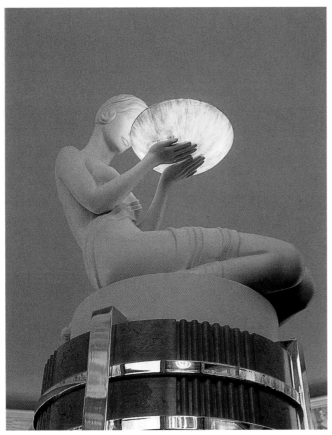

The internal glow emitted from the bronzed bowls is produced by neon ring (above left) **and dimmed incandescent light** (above right).

The second aspect of the project was the Gateway of Entertainment, a 170-foot diameter entry dome. 'The charge was to create a room evocative of another era – one of soft, warm light, glowing edifices, and film and theatre spectacle – all by way of the architecture and light,' explains De Alessi. The effect was achieved with a combination of concealed indirect lighting and a series of decorative fittings.

The bas-relief panels which encircle the room on both sides of the entablature ring and the grille below (housing sound reinforcement) were both uplit from concealed cove-mounted 5W and 10W xenon low-voltage strip lights, dimmed to produce the warm colour associated with the deco period and to extend lamp life. Above the entablature ring, Lalique crystal panels are uplit on the relief side from recessed adjustable MR16 fittings mounted flush in the ring's top. This also allows the dome colour to glow through one side while reinforcing the panel's sculptural qualities.

The mural which encircles the dome is again uplit, with three rows of dimmable curvilinear cold cathode lamps in pink, gold and pale blue, also cove-mounted and concealed. A snap-on reflector gives better control and efficiency while customised radial louvres were made to restrict light output from all coves to the entablatures and murals to avoid muddying or muting the rich ceiling colour. The ceiling itself is a canvas for 52 moving mirror fittings with dichroic colour filters and gobos.

Decorative luminaires either have diffused neon rings or dimmed incandescent lamps for life and colour. Most of them also have baffles on the top, both to prevent glare to people at balcony level and to preserve the integrity of the ceiling colour. A diffused neon ring uplights the kneeling statue's face in a soft glow, while ambient light only illuminates the body. Other statues are accented with recessed MR16 fittings using simple white light to differentiate them from backgrounds.

'Lighting played an important role in art deco-period architecture, as it created truly luminous environments, calling attention to façade and feature and not the lighting system itself. This feeling is recreated here,' says De Alessi.

Pflaums Posthotel, Pegnitz, Germany
Architect, interior designer, lighting designer: Dirk Obliers Design

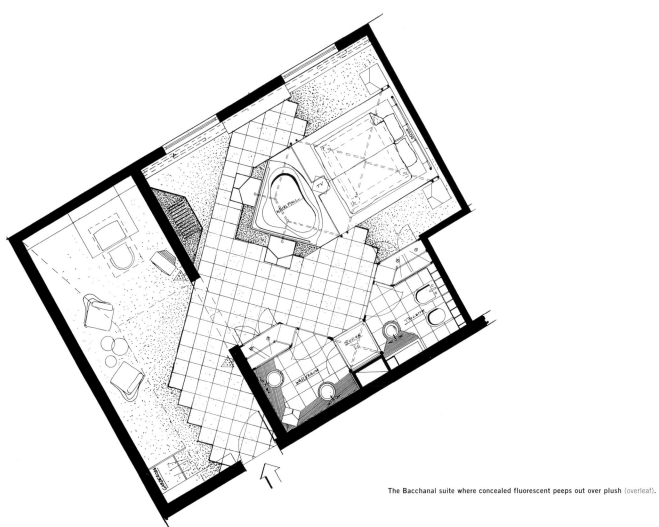

The Bacchanal suite where concealed fluorescent peeps out over plush (overleaf).

'The most important thing is not the fitting as an object but the effect of light.'

Few hotels are guaranteed to startle the unwary guest more than Pflaums in southern Germany. The exterior of the 300-year-old hotel, all half-timber and geraniums, is Bavarian vernacular at its most typical and twee. This is a highly misleading introduction: the interior is flamboyant, experimental and not so much theatrical as operatic (appropriately enough as it is a homage to Wagner whose world-famous festival takes place at nearby Beyreuth).

The Bacchanal (above), the Klingsor's Fairygarden Suite (facing top left), the Venus in Blue Suite (facing top right), the Parsifal Suite (facing centre left), the Blue Corridor (facing centre right) and the Tristan Suite (facing bottom right and left).

The schemes for each of the individually designed 25 luxury suites veer from red plush bordello to techno-kitsch with slightly more orthodox contemporary somewhere in between. Dirk Obliers views them as stage sets and considers the lighting to be an integral part of his design vision. 'Light for me is very, very important – it is key in creating the design of the room. At the beginning of the planning, when I am developing a new solution, it is very important to have the lighting effect in my mind.'

Luminaires are sometimes visible and occasionally contribute as decorative elements. In the Klingsor's Fairygarden Suite, for example, Artemide's classic Tizio is on show and three light strips radiate from the bedhead as magic wands. In the White Suite handkerchief-style halogen fittings are attached to the ceiling. Where they do occur they are primarily specially designed by Obliers; but his main concern is not with the luminaire but light itself. Frequently the source is concealed altogether. 'The most important thing is not the fitting as an object but the effect of light.'

Obliers uses three main sources: fluorescent and fibre optics for special effects, and halogen for downlighting and highlighting. 'I like to play with these three lighting elements in different ways,' he says. Outside the ballroom, rarely do fibre optics find such flamboyant application in the hotel environment as they do in the Parsifal Suite. The sleeping cave area is partly defined by a black sky dotted with light points as stars. Even more spectacularly, fibre optics are combined with mirrors to create an infinity effect in the 'light tunnel' which links the indoor golf area with the pool.

Fluorescent is characteristically used for indirect lighting in the golf area, casting a blue glow on the wall. The source is a blue tube. The same concept is repeated in another passage, the 'Blue Corridor', where three square decorative elements use either fluorescent or fibre optics to show the playful effects of light. 'Light planning and design are not limited to the technical function and application of conventional lamps, but go beyond to an unequivocally aesthetic dimension,' says Obliers.

Jumeirah Beach Resort Development,
Dubai, UAE
Lighting designer (exterior and selected interior spaces): Jonathan Speirs and Associates
Architect: WS Atkins

PHOTOGRAPH © JSA

The heavily glazed exterior of the Jumeirah Beach (facing and above) **meant a straightforward lighting solution was not possible.**

The flagship resort in Dubai's bid to become the leading holiday destination in the Gulf, the Jumeirah Beach Resort Development is a complex of two hotels, an aqua park, conference centre, sports centre and numerous restaurants. JSA created lighting schemes for most of these components, including the extensive landscaping, but it is the two hotels which make the rather more overt statements at night, transformed by a vibrant and vivid lighting show, they blaze in their desert setting.

On the seaward side (above and facing), the lower level white wall became a canvas for a constantly changing artwork using Irideon colour projectors. On the landward side, a blue wash was created using metal halide floods with blue filters (overleaf).

'The general principles were to create magic, excitement, fun, interest, mood and drama.'

The Burj Al Arab (Arabian Tower), 300 metres high and with 202 duplex suites, is the more exclusive of the two hotels, while the Jumeirah Beach, 100 metres high and with 600 guest rooms, is aimed at a wider market. In both cases, the approach to the lighting is bold. 'The general principles were to create magic, excitement, fun, interest, mood and drama,' says Alan Mitchell of JSA.

The exterior of the Jumeirah is primarily glass which meant that a straightforward lighting solution was not possible. The land side was lit with 90 1,000W HQI floodlights in various beam widths and fitted with blue glass filters. This created a blue wash on the spandrel panels between the glazing. On the seaward side, a white wall at the lower level for balconies became the canvas for a constantly changing artwork using 29 Irideon automated colour wash luminaires in recessed pits. For extra pizazz, strobe lights are positioned in the spandrel panels on both elevations and are automatically activated every 15 minutes for 90 seconds. 'It creates the effect of many tiny sparkles across the whole façade, like hundreds of Japanese tourists taking pictures at the same time,' says Mitchell.

The exterior lighting for the Burj Al Arab is concentrated on the 180 metre high Teflon-coated element.

The extent of the glazing was also a constraint where the Burj Al Arab was concerned. An extraordinary architectural statement, the resort's prestigious showpiece hotel is built on a man-made island and evokes a boat's mast caught in the wind. The huge trusses in the ground-breaking structure allowed a large proportion of the surface to be glazed enabling stunning views from the suites. The third elevation comprises double-skinned, Teflon-coated woven glass fibre (the largest use of such materials in any building worldwide). In order to resolve the expanse of glazing, the majority of the lighting is concentrated on this 180 metre high fabric element. Irideon colour change luminaires (60 located on the bridge leading to the island and 20 on the island abutment) were again used to achieve the primary effect. Starting with white light, the luminaires change every 15 minutes. A more kinetic two- to three-minute lighting show takes place each hour when the lights change colour and wash up, down and across the screen.

On either side of the screen, 40 High End AF1000 strobes are positioned on the exoskeleton legs supporting the main structure. These also come on at various times to form different patterns: strobing, flashing, running up and down either side. At the top of the tower there are a further 58 Irideons complementing the screen with changing colour washes. At the pinnacle are four Sky Tracker 7Kw units which throw a pencil beam of light into the sky that can be seen for miles around. In a final *Bladerunner* touch, four PIGI 7,000W scrolling projectors allow for large format images to be projected on to the fabric screen. These can move from side to side and have a total area size of 120 x 40 metres. Mounted 300 metres away on the land opposite the tower, they represent the longest throw of any permanent installation of its kind in the world.

Given the amount of activity on the tower, restraint is shown elsewhere – the sides are lit simply with white light, as is the surrounding landscape, so that the structure remains firmly delineated, outstanding in all senses.

section three

Light is fundamental to our existence and to our perception of our world. It is a life-giving force fuelling processes such as photosynthesis that allow flora and fauna to survive and thrive. It reveals our environment to us; it warms us; it affects our mood and sense of well-being. It is a metaphor for understanding – we are enlightened – and even for divine revelation – 'we see the light'. And yet for centuries thinkers and scientists from Aristotle to Sir Isaac Newton have wrestled to understand the nature of light. 'I was so persecuted with discussions arising out of my theory of light, that I blame my own impudence for parting with so substantial a blessing to run after a shadow,' declared Newton.

400 450 500 550 600 650 700

WAVELENGTHS

ɔectrum.

Light

ɔ define it technically, light is the part of the ᵉctromagnetic spectrum which can be seen by the ɪman eye. It is visible energy. Within that narrow band ɪbetween 400 and 800 nanometres in wavelength – the ᵉ can distinguish a range of colours from red (the ɔrtest wavelength) to blue. Either side of this band is ɪfrared and ultraviolet.

ɪe primary source of light is the sun – directly during ᵉ day and indirectly from the moon at night, ɪpplemented by starlight. Although sunlight changes in ɪtensity and colour depending on weather conditions ɪd the geographical position of the observer, it is still ɪr yardstick when it comes to judging lighting effects.

ʰen fire was discovered, mankind stumbled across the ʳst artificial light. Oil lamps and candles, both of which ɪɪt a redder, warmer light than the sun, were the only ɪtificial light sources for millennia until the emergence ˈ new techniques in the 19th century – first gas lighting ɪd then in 1880, the electric lamp. Both Thomas Edison the USA and Sir Joseph Swan in Britain can lay claim developing the first incandescent electric lamp, a fact knowledged by their subsequently founding a joint ɪmpany.

ɪther as horsepower persists somewhat redundantly as unit of measurement for the combustion engine, the ʳm foot-candle is still used in the USA as a way of ᵉasuring the power of a source to emit light.

Colour

Scientists believe that human beings can differentiat᎓ between some 40 million colours. But that conclusion i᎓ not finite in the sense that the number of colours a᎓ individual can perceive will depend on the receptivity o᎓ the rods and cones in his or her eye (rods detect th᎓ intensity of the light, while cones analyse the colour o᎓ objects into a mixture of red, yellow and blue tints).

There is also an element of subjectivity – how man᎓ people have argued over whether an object is blue o᎓ green? The picture is further complicated by socia᎓ conditioning which invests certain colours wit᎓ psychological effects.

The relationship between light and colour is comple᎓ and the two are inextricably intertwined. The 'white᎓ light we perceive is in fact composed of the complet᎓ range of colours, the spectrum, as Sir Isaac Newto᎓ discovered when he passed a beam of light through ᵃ prism, and as even the non-scientific can observe in th᎓ arc of a rainbow.

The interplay of light and colour is a crucial aspect o᎓ lighting design.

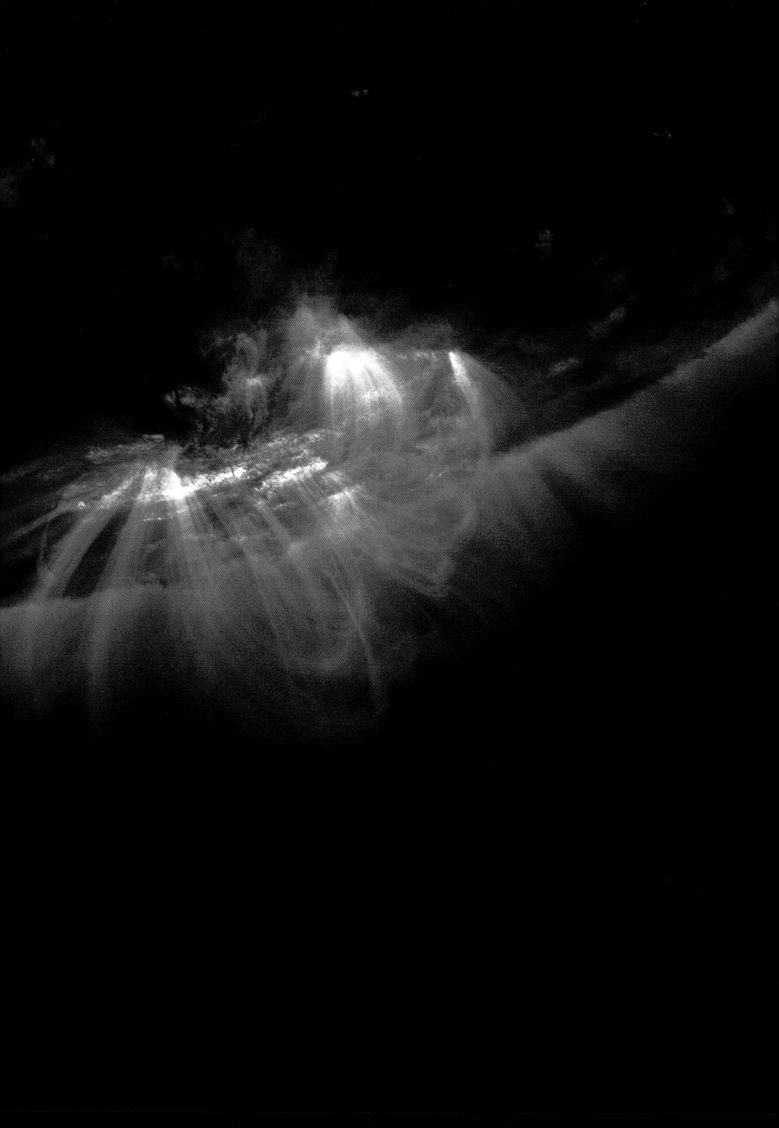

Natural light shows fruit in its most colourful beauty – as our eye would see it in nature.

Fluorescent with a high colour rendering index (CRI) shows all the colours with a slight bluish appearance.

White son (high pressure sodium) has a strong red but appears very natural.

Colour rendering

When white light strikes a coloured object, the surface of the object absorbs part of the spectrum and reflects the rest according to its colour. In other words, a red object absorbs all wavelengths of light except red, which is why we see it as red in a white light. But if the original light is not colour balanced – very few light sources, natural or artificial, emit the whole range of colours in equal proportions – it will affect the perceived colour of the object.

A red object seen in a blue light appears black, for instance, because there is no red light to reflect. Or consider low pressure sodium street lighting – the yellow light is sufficient to allow parked cars to be discernible as shapes, but it is extremely difficult to determine what colour they are.

The physical quality of an object's surface is also a key factor. Different surfaces have their own colour values (the range of the spectrum they will absorb or reflect) and different reflectance values (the amount of light – whatever colour – they reflect). All lamps have an Ra rating to indicate their colour rendering.

Metal halide loses some appearance in red but still gives good colour rendering.

Fluorescent with a low CRI has poor colour rendering especially at the red end of the spectrum. PHOTOGRAPHS BY BOB YOUNG.

Colour rendering groups	Colour rendering index	Typical application
1A	Ra>90	Wherever accurate colour matching is required, e.g. colour printing inspection.
1B	90>Ra>80	Wherever accurate colour judgements are necessary or good colour rendering is required for reasons of appearance, e.g. shops. Appropriate for most hotel spaces and the minimum recommended for a bar/restaurant environment.
2	80<Ra<60	Wherever moderate colour rendering is required.
3	60<Ra<40	Wherever colour rendering is of little significance but marked distortion of colour is unacceptable.
4	40<Ra<20	Wherever colour rendering is of no importance at all and marked distortion of colour is acceptable.

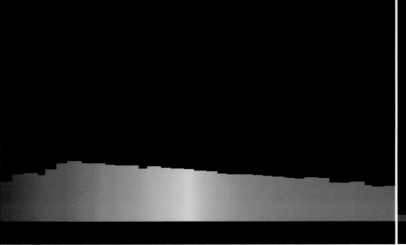

400   500   600   700n

The spectral composition of natural daylight.

Typical spectral composition of an incandescent lamp showing its bias towards the red end of the spectrum.

Colour temperature

While all light sources broadly speaking emit 'white light' (with the obvious exceptions such as coloured lamps), it clearly varies according to the type of lamp. The traditional incandescent lamp found in most homes creates a warm glow at the reddish end of the spectrum.

The fluorescent lamp in the office produces a cooler effect. This variance is measured in colour temperature, specifically degrees Kelvin.

If a strip of metal is heated, it first turns red, then yellow, then blue and finally blue white. Its temperature at any stage can be measured in degrees Kelvin. So 3,000K is very warm (incandescent lamps are between 2,600–3,200K), 6,000K is very cool (an overcast sky is around 6,500K). Despite the psychological association of the sun with warmth, daylight is extremely cool. A cloudless summer day would have a colour temperature of 10,000K.

Any lighting scheme therefore needs to take into account the colour of surface materials and objects, their reflectance and the colour temperature of the lamps specified.

Working with United Designers, Box Products used arts and crafts and art deco influences for lighting throughout Dublin's 1930s' Clarence hotel, owned by band U2 (facing).

Fluorescent overhead lighting fails to flatter the vase.

A single overhead pin spot produces a degree of sparkle.

A high degree of brilliance with sparkle is achieved by combining the pin spot with an accent spot and flair beam lighting (wider symmetrical beam bordering on a flood) from behind.

Visual effect

As already discussed, the colour of the light can have a radical effect on how an object is seen. The same is also true of the spread of light and the angle at which it strikes an object. A face lit solely from above looks dramatically different from one lit from below. An object needs more than ambient lighting to realise its decorative potential. In order to flatter a face or bring out the true beauty of an object, lighting needs to be balanced.

The mask has been photographed lit by a single, very oblique spot, in each case from a different direction. The effects of the changing location of the light source range from spooky to threatening. It demonstrates that a balance between diffuse and directional lighting is the optimum solution for lighting the human face – especially when it's across a reception desk or restaurant table (facing).

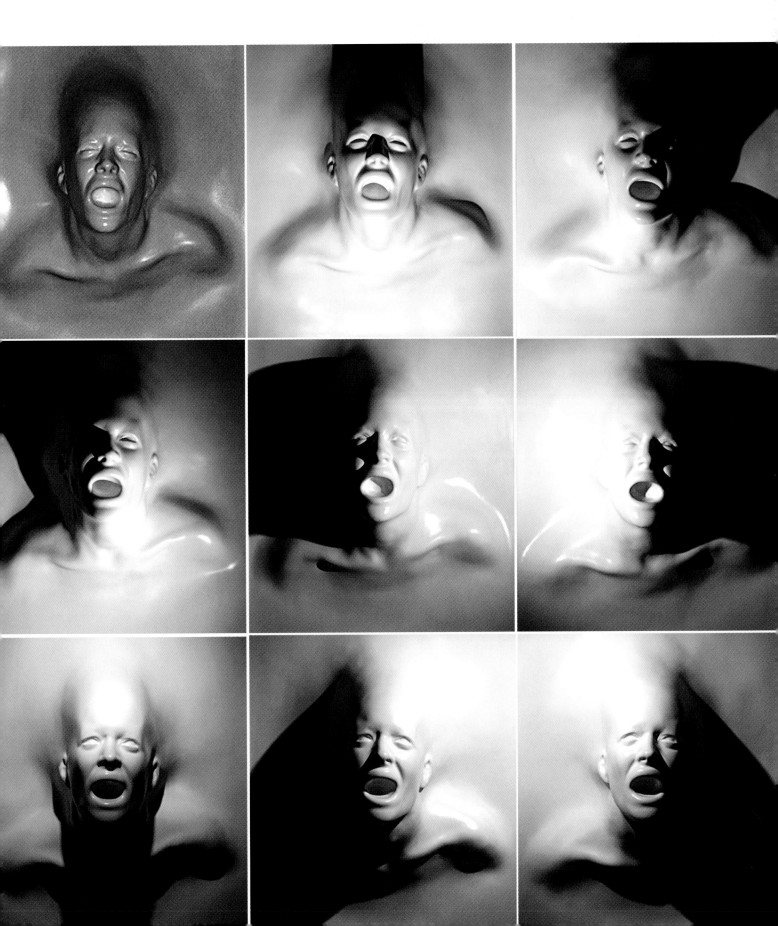

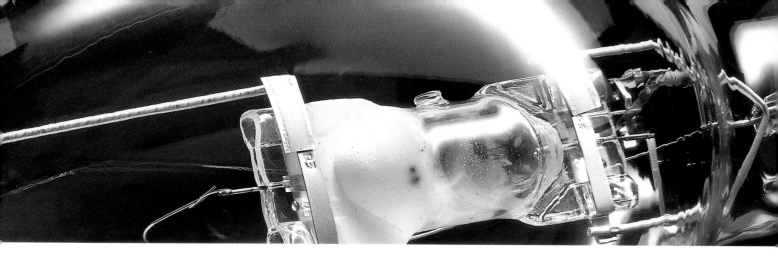

Artificial light

Selecting the appropriate equipment (lamp, fitting and, where appropriate, control gear such as a transformer), involves a number of considerations. Some are practical – light output, efficiency and cost – and some are aesthetic – light distribution, intensity and diffusion. The solution will usually involve devising a system that uses different lamps and fittings to achieve an overall effect.

Output

The amount of light emitted by a lamp is measured in lumens (Europe) or candela (USA). Typical values for different lamp types can be found in the chart on page 151. Manufacturers will supply more precise calculations.

Efficiency

This refers to the proportion of energy consumed by a lamp that is emitted as light and to its ability to maintain a consistent output. The traditional incandescent lamp, for instance, is extremely inefficient because 95 per cent of the energy it produces is given off as heat. At the end of its life it delivers only 80 per cent of its initial lumen output.

Cost

Expenditure on lighting equipment and its installation is clearly the primary consideration. However, it can be overemphasised at the expense of the second consideration of running costs – electrical consumption and maintenance. A fluorescent lamp, for example, will consume less electricity and will have a longer life if it is run by an initially more expensive high frequency electronic ballast than a cheaper conventional model. In most hotel spaces, especially areas such as the lobby, bars, restaurants and lounge areas, aesthetics generally rate more highly than practicality, but back of house is not necessarily the only area which could benefit from a long-term rather than short-term view.

Light distribution

It is the lamp and the fitting together which determine how light is distributed. Certain lamps will have inbuilt reflectors and diffusers, while fittings will vary in terms of lenses, reflectors and other techniques to control the direction and intensity of the output. Manufacturers' product information will usually show the distribution pattern of a particular fitting in a 'polar curve' diagram.

Intensity

The amount of light falling on a surface or an object is called illuminance and is measured in lux (lumens per square metre). While less relevant in a hotel context, there are guidelines governing desirable lux levels in different environments, some of which are linked to official regulations.

Diffusion

The overall level of lighting achieved by a scheme and easily calculated by a wide range of computer programmes.

From left to right: standard mains voltage incandescent lamp with a silvered crown, PAR 20 tungsten mains voltage, PAR 30 tungsten mains voltage, halogen GZ10.

Lamps

For practical purposes lamps are grouped into three categories: incandescent, fluorescent (including compact fluorescent lamps or CFLs) and discharge, though strictly speaking fluorescent is also a form of discharge lamp.

Lamps are classified according to the electrical system used to create light – either by passing a current through a wire filament (incandescent) or through an envelope filled with reactive gas (discharge). There are thousands of different lamps – the following is an outline of key sources.

Incandescent

The progenitors of all electric lighting, these lamps work on the filament principle – an electric current causes the wire to glow, or incandesce, when it reaches a certain temperature.

• *Tungsten GLS (general lighting service) lamp:* Its 'warm' colour makes it perennially popular, especially for domestic use, despite its short life and relative inefficiency.

• *PAR lamp:* With an integral parabolic reflector, it allows far greater directional control. It also lasts about twice as long as a GLS lamp.

• *Tungsten halogen:* Introduced in the 1950s, the lamps have a light quality closer to daylight and (because of the halogen gas which inhibits deterioration of the filament) a longer life than tungsten incandescent.

Mains voltage: Available in linear and PAR versions, the most recent development is the low voltage lookalike. It has less punch but the advantage of no transformer.

Low voltage: Available in capsule and reflector versions, they offer a lot of pluses – excellent colour rendering, small lamp sizes, good beam control, long life and low operating costs. It is important, however, to have a good transformer (preferably one which compensates for voltage fluctuations) and to ensure correct installation.

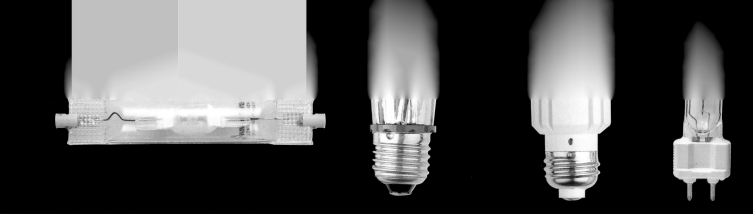

From left to right: double ended mains voltage, two types of PAR 20 halogen (electronic on the right), CDM-T Mastercolour.

Fluorescent

An electrical current passed through a gas or vapour excites mercury atoms which release ultraviolet light. A phosphor coating on the glass tube reacts to the UV radiation and fluoresces, producing visible light. In recent years, using a triple coating of phosphor (triphosphor) has improved the colour rendering of what is a highly efficient, long life source.

• *Tube:* The recent narrower tube, T5 (16mm), has spawned a range of elegant contemporary fittings. The pencil slim T2 can be used for shelf lighting. With coloured sleeves or gels, they can be a cheap but highly effective source for concealed lighting, wallwashing and backlighting.

• *Compact:* The variety of lamp shapes and sizes made possible by bending narrow fluorescent tubes has brought style to low energy in a vast range of luminaires of all types. The light intensity of the higher wattage lamps makes them ideal for illuminating large spaces.

Discharge

Developed in the 1930s and highly efficient, it is only recently that more exciting advances have been made in discharge lamps and their use become more widespread in interior applications. High intensity discharge lamps (HID) are based on sodium (orange white light) or mercury (bluish colour) vapour. All lamps require control gear.

• *Ceramic metal halide:* While conventional metal halide, based on quartz technology, has always been associated with shifts in colour temperature, the use of a ceramic arc tube solved the problem in the early 90s. The range of wattages and options on colour temperature/rendering has steadily increased and this has become an extremely popular lamp, especially for retail display.

• *Cold cathode:* Low voltage, easily dimmable and with a very long life (by the book, 45,000 hours but often 100,000 hours), cold cathode has considerable potential as a concealed or overtly decorative source.

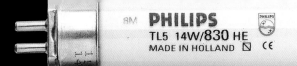

the slimline 16mm or T5 fluorescent tube.

Summary guide to main lamp types

	Type	Wattage	Life in hours	Colour temperature
Mains voltage (240 volts) tungsten	Standard GLS	25–200 watt	1,000	2,700
	General purpose incandescent with good colour reproduction.			
	Reflector lamps	25–150 watt	1,000	2,700
	Mirror reflective coating on the inside of the lamp creates directional light in an uniform beam at angles between 25 (narrow) and 80 (broad) degrees.			
	PAR 38	60–120 watt	2,000–2,500	2,700
	Controlled light dispersal (12–30 degree beam angle) with high mechanical strength.			
Mains voltage (240 volts) halogen	Capsule	75–300 watt	1,500–4,000	2,900
	Quartz halogen lamps for high output (luminous flux up to 5,000).			
	Standard halogen	75–100 watt	2,000	2,900
	Much whiter light than standard incandescent with double the lamp life.			
	Halogen PAR 20	50 watt	2,000–5,000	2,900
	Halogen PAR 30	75–100 watt	2,500	2,900
	Halogen PAR 38	75–150 watt	2,500	2,900
	Can replace standard PAR or reflector lamps with higher output halogen.			
	Double ended	150–500 watt	2,000	2,800–2,950
	Luminous flux up to 9,500 from a double-ended tube.			
	Low voltage lookalikes	40–75 watt	2,000-2,500	2,700–2,850
	Available in both aluminium reflector and dichroic versions.			
Mains voltage (240 volts) fluorescent	Tubular fluorescent	4–125 watt	6,000–20,000	2,500–6,000
	Colour temperature depends on lamp colour.			
	Triphosphor fluorescent	18–125 watt	6,000–20,000	6,500
	Triphosphor lamps are recommended for applications where accurate colour values are necessary.			
Mains voltage (240 volts) compact fluorescent	CFL retrofit	5–23 watt	6,000–12,000	2,700–4,000
	Compacts offer the advantages of tubular fluorescent in a smaller format.			
	CFL non-retrofit	5–55 watt	8,000–16,000	2,700–4,000
	These lamps require starter gear.			
Low voltage (12 volts) halogen	QT	20–100 watt	2,000–3,000	2,900
	Compact dimensions with good output and colour rendering.			
	Dichroic: open front	20–75 watt	2,000–3,000	2,900
	closed front	20–75 watt	3,000–5,000	2,900
	Well-defined beam (angles 8–60 degrees), excellent colour rendition, especially useful in food and heat sensitive contexts as 70 per cent of heat generated is radiated backwards.			
	Metal reflector	15–50 watt	2,000	2,900
	Aluminium reflector lamps with precisely directed beam (angles 6–32 degrees).			
High intensity discharge mains voltage (240 volts)	Metal halide	35watt–2kilowatt	5,000	3,000–5,600
	Good output with low colour rendering, require starter gear.			
	PAR 38	35–100 watt	9,000	3,000
	Metal halide lamp with PAR integral reflector.			
	SON	50watt–1kilowatt	12,000	1,950–2,150
	Output equivalent to standard GLS lamp.			
	CDM	35–150 watt	9,000	3,000

Luminaires

However decorative in appearance, the luminaire or light fitting is about much more than aesthetics. In fact it performs a number of functions – it enables the electrical connection to the lamp itself, it protects the lamp and it directs or diffuses the light from the lamp.

Luminaires can broadly be divided into the following categories: downlights, uplights, wall lights, spotlights, ceiling-mounted, suspended and recessed fittings. Then there are portable luminaires such as table and floor-standing lamps. However, many sophisticated fittings can be used in alternative positions and often combine categories – an up/downlight, for example.

Some fittings will take a range of lamps (supplied according to specification) and a spotlight will often accommodate lamps with different beam widths.

The hotel environment clearly offers infinite decorative possibilities and great potential for customisation, especially with feature fittings such as large-scale chandeliers for lobbies and ballrooms.

Table lamp from the Foyer range of ceramic lamps by Chelsom for public areas and **prestige bedrooms** (above). COURTESY OF CHELSOM.

Canterbury chandelier (facing). COURTESY OF LOCKINGTON.

present trends
and
future

section four

update

We tend to associate individuality in hotels with the small characterful establishment which has often started life in some other guise – the crumbling colonial villa in Macau, the former monastery in Lisbon, the modest maharaja's palace in Jaipur, the charming converted cottages in the Cotswolds.

Today hotels are no longer reliant on the past for personality. Boutique hotels can be bolder with their narrowly targeted niche audiences, but even larger operators, constrained by a wider, more conservative clientele, are less fearful of upsetting guests by straying too far from the neutral palette of tradition.

The phenomenon of the business traveller, the massive increase in tourism and intense competition in the travel industry have led to a re-evaluation of what the guest wants and what the hotel can offer. That in turn has led to a greater attention to detail on the one hand and an increasingly stimulating environment on the other.

Inevitably this process has had implications for lighting. On a detailed level the guest room itself has come under more scrutiny – the introduction of appropriate task lighting for business people, discreet reading lamps, the use of nightlights. The potential for improvement is still great, however. Simple dimming systems – possibly controlled by their integration into the remote controls used for TV and video – would be an enormous step forward and it is only a matter of time before they become more widespread.

Elsewhere lighting is becoming more integrated, more

project, the lighting is forming a more complex element within it,' says Sally Storey of Lighting Design International. 'At the same time one is rationalising it to simplify the maintenance.'

In design terms, the incorporation of more unusual materials is also increasing the parameters of possible lighting effects. 'Spaces are becoming so much more stimulating and different,' says Maurice Brill of Maurice Brill Lighting Design. 'The use of materials such as glass for flooring, which lends itself so well to lighting, can make a huge difference to a scheme.'

The future of hotel lighting, for interiors and exteriors, is both colourful and inspirational. Unusual lighting effects will be less limited to the resort and casino venue, and while more discreetly translated, will permeate into a broader spectrum of hotels. 'At the moment it's more in the contemporary hotel, but colour is being increasingly used,' says Sally Storey. 'It's definitely evident even in floodlighting to the point, for instance, of saturating some trees in colour, which you could get away with even at a more traditional hotel.' 'More acceptance of colour and more integrated feature lighting has become the norm,' says Brill. 'I think projection, colour and theatre are high on the

Glossary

Accent lighting: Lighting that directs visual focus to a particular object, element or space.

Adaptation: The process which takes place as the visual system adjusts itself to different brightness ranges or colour (chromatic adaptation). The term is also used, usually qualified, to denote the final stage of this process.

Ambient lighting: The general level of lighting in a space.

Apparent colour: Of a light source; subjectively the hue of the source or of a white surface illuminated by the source; the degree of warmth associated with the source colour. Lamps of low correlated colour temperatures are usually described as having a warm apparent colour, and lamps of high correlated colour temperature as having a cold apparent colour.

Average illuminance (Eave): The arithmetic mean illuminance over the specified surface.

Baffle: A device which can be attached to a fitting to shield a lamp from view, to prevent glare or to direct a beam of light.

Brightness: The subjective response to luminance in the field of view dependent upon the adaptation of the eye. Differing from luminance, which is measured by a light meter.

Candela (cd): The SI unit of luminous intensity, equal to one lumen per steradian.

Chroma: In the Munsell system, an index of saturation of colour ranging from 0 for neutral grey to 10 or over for strong colours. A low chroma implies a pastel shade.

Colour constancy: The condition resulting from the process of chromatic adaptation whereby the colour of objects is not perceived to change greatly under a wide range of lighting conditions both in terms of colour quality and luminance.

Colour rendering: A general expression for the appearance of surface colours when illuminated by light from a given source compared, consciously or unconsciously, with their appearance under light from some reference source. Good colour rendering implies similarity of appearance to that under an acceptable light source, such as daylight. Typical areas requiring good or excellent colour rendering are quality control areas and laboratories where colour evaluation takes place.

Colour temperature: How cool or warm the appearance of a lamp is. Measured in degrees Kelvin.

Contrast: A term that is used subjectively and objectively. Subjectively it describes the difference in appearance of two parts of a visual field seen simultaneously or successively. The difference may be one of brightness or colour, or both. Objectively, the term expresses the luminance difference between the two parts of the field.

Control system: An increasingly essential facility ranging from simple dimming to systems with presence detection and daylight control.

Cut-off angle: The angle above which no light is emitted.

Dichroic mirror: Glass which has special coatings and is used as a filter that selectively reflects some wavelengths while transmitting others.

Diffuse reflection: Reflection in which the reflected light is diffused and there is no significant specular reflection, as from a matt paint.

Diffuser: A device, usually part of a light fitting, by which light is softened and scattered.

Directional lighting: Lighting designed to illuminate a task or surface predominantly from one direction.

Discharge lamp: A lamp in which the light is produced either directly or by the excitation of phosphors by an electric discharge through a gas, a metal vapour or a mixture of several gases and vapours.

Downlighter: Direct lighting luminaires from which light is emitted only within relatively small angles to the downward vertical.

Efficacy: The ratio of lumens produced to the power (watts) consumed by the lamp.

Fluorescent lamp: This category of lamps functions by converting ultraviolet energy (created by an electrical discharge in mercury vapour) into visible light through interaction with the phosphor coating of the tube.

Glare: The discomfort or impairment of vision experienced when parts of the visual field are excessively bright in relation to the general surroundings.

Hue: Colour in the sense of red, or yellow or green etc. (See also Munsell.)

Illuminance (E, units: lm/m2, lux): The amount of light falling on to a surface. Formerly known as the illumination value or illumination level.

Incandescent lamp: A lamp in which light is produced by a filament heated to incandescence by the passage of an electric current.

Indirect lighting: The method by which light is reflected from, say, ceilings and walls before reaching the plane of interest.

Lamp: The source of artificial light and referred to as a bulb by the non-lighting fraternity.

Lumen (lm): The SI unit of luminous flux, used in describing a quantity of light emitted by a source or received by a surface. A small source which has a uniform luminous intensity of one candela emits a total of 4 x pi lumens in all directions and emits one lumen within a unit solid angle, i.e. one steradian.

Luminaire: The term used by the lighting profession to describe a light fitting.

Luminance: The amount of light coming off a surface. It depends on the reflection factor of the surface and the amount of light falling on to that surface.

Lux (lux): The SI unit of illuminance, equal to one lumen per square metre (lm/m2).

Munsell system: A system of surface colour classification using uniform colour scales of hue, value and chroma. A typical Munsell designation of a colour is 7.5 BG6/2, where 7.5 BG (blue green) is the hue reference, 6 is the value and 2 is the chroma reference number.

Optical radiation: That part of the electromagnetic spectrum from 100nm to 1nm.

Reflectance (factor) (R, p): The ratio of light reflected from a surface to light incident on it. Except for matt surfaces, reflectance depends on how the surface is illuminated but especially on the direction of the incident light and its spectral distribution.

Saturation: The subjective estimate of the amount of pure chromatic colour present in a sample, judged in proportion to its brightness.

Specular: Very smooth, mirror-like surface used, for instance, for luminaire louvres and other reflectors.

Spill light: The light which is cast outside the main beam, falling unwantedly on to other objects and surfaces.

Uplighter: Luminaires which direct most of the light upwards on to the ceiling or upper walls in order to illuminate the working plane by reflection.

Utilisation factor (UF): The proportion of luminous flux emitted by lamps which reaches the working plane.

Working plane: The horizontal, vertical, or inclined plane in which the visual task lies. If no information is available, the working plane may be considered to be horizontal and at 0.8m above the floor.

Further information

Publications

C. Gardner & B. Hannaford, *Lighting Design*, (Design Council, 1993)

J. Turner, *Lighting, an Introduction to Light, Lighting and Light Use*, (Batsford, 1994)

J. Turner, *Designing with Light. Retail Spaces: Lighting Solutions for Shops, Malls and Markets*, (RotoVision SA, 1998)

J. Turner, *Designing with Light. Public Places: Lighting Solutions for Exhibitions, Museums and Historic Spaces*, (RotoVision SA, 1998)

J. Entwistle, *Designing with Light. Bars and Restaurants*, (RotoVision SA, 1999)

Good Lighting for Restaurants and Hotels
Fordergemeinschaft Gutes Licht
Stresemannallee 19
D-6000 Frankfurt/M.70
Germany
Tel: +49 69 63 02-0
Fax: +49 69 63 02-317

Code for Interior Lighting
Chartered Institute of Building Services Engineers (CIBSE) Lighting Division
Delta House
222 Balham High Road
London SW12 9BS
UK
Tel: +44 20 8675 5211
Fax: +44 20 8675 5449

Lighting bodies

International Association of Lighting Designers
Suite 487
The Merchandise Mart
200 World Trade Center
Chicago, IL 60654
USA
Tel: +1 312 527 3677
Fax: +1 312 527 3680
E-mail: iald@iald.org
Website: www.iald.org

IALD UK
Lennox House
9 Lawford Road
Rugby
Warwickshire CV21 2DZ
UK
Tel/Fax: +44 1788 570 760
E-mail: iald@iald.org
Website: www.iald.org

European Lighting Designers Association (ELDA)
Postfach 3201
D-33262 Gutersloh
Germany
Tel: +49 5241 92900
Fax: +49 5241 92938
E-mail: via-verlag@t-online.de

Index